BRITTANY'S

GREEN
WAYS

Old railway tracks and canal towpaths
across Brittany

A guide for cyclists and walkers

by

G H Randall

Brittany's Green Ways
2nd edition
published by Red Dog Books
ISBN 978 0 9568699 6 8

© Red Dog Books 2014

(1st edition published in 2010. Reprinted 2011, 2012)

British Library Cataloguing-in-Publication Data
A catalogue record for this book is available from the British Library

Red Dog Books is based in Somerset and in Brittany.
Enquiries should be addressed to the editorial office at
Red Dog Books, 29410 Plounéour-Ménez, France.

email: reddogbooks@orange.fr

www.reddogbooks.com

Printed and bound in China

CONTENTS

INTRODUCTION

"Communication routes reserved exclusively for non-motorised journeys, developed in an integrated manner which enhances both the environment and quality of life of the surrounding area. These routes should meet satisfactory standards of width, gradient, and surface condition to ensure that they are both user-friendly and low-risk for users of all abilities"

Declaration of Lille - working definition of Green Ways.

This guide book has its origins in the emergence of Green Ways, *voies vertes*, stemming from the 'Declaration of Lille' in 2000. That declaration's working definition of a Green Way still serves to distinguish proper Green Ways from other cycling routes which have cropped up in their wake. The Association Européenne des Voies Vertes (AEVV) enlarges on it a little: "Greenways are transport corridors, developed along independent routes following past or disused communication pathways and tracks that are available for non-motorised soft traffic". It is this aspect of using old railway lines and canal towpaths that gives the Green Ways one of their key elements - "...low or zero gradient, allowing their use by all types of user, including mobility impaired people."

By and large, that is what the Green Ways of Brittany are - old railway lines and canal towpaths, developed and enhanced with signage, a stabilised surface and secured road crossings.

ROUTES

Because there are so many of these 'disused communication pathways' in Brittany, and they can stretch for a considerable distance, they form the basis of a system of cycle routes, that is loosely referred to as 'the Green Ways', or *'voies vertes'*. But it would be wrong to assume that any of these routes are entirely along Green Ways. Some sections may be less user friendly - signed along quiet but not entirely traffic-free roads, for example, with perhaps a few steep hills.

In Brittany these routes are known by a number together with their starting point and destination:

The V1 - Roscoff to Nantes
The V2 - St-Malo to Arzal
The V3 - St-Malo to Rhuys
The V4/5 - La Littorale (around the coast - still incomplete and very little of it is Green Way)
The V6 - Camaret to Vitré
The V7 - Roscoff to Concarneau
The V8 - St-Brieuc to Lorient

The names can be misleading. Firstly, it is best to think of the 'V' as standing for *'voie vélo'* (bicycle way) rather than *'voie verte'* (Green Way) and they encompass the whole of Brittany, crossing department boundaries. Secondly, the starting point and destination express a long term plan rather than a present reality. The V3, for example, starts in Dinard rather than St-Malo and stops a long way short of the Presqu'île de Rhuys. The V6 is a fully joined-up and signed route only between Pont Triffen (on the Nantes-Brest Canal 11kms west of Port de Carhaix) and St-Méen-le-Grand. The V7, as a continuous Green Way, starts from Morlaix (although it is signed by minor roads from Roscoff), and south of Rosporden it is on a signed route of minor roads and tracks finishing a few kilometres short of Concarneau.

Further confusion can arise from different names applied to the same route. The V1 Roscoff - Nantes, for example, is a section of the Ev1 (European Cyclists' Federation's 'Eurovélo Atlantic Coast' route from the North Cape in Norway to Sagres in Portugal). The French section of Ev1 was completed in 2012, linked with a route in Devon and dubbed *Velodyssey*. Similarly, the first section, Brittany, of the European Cyclists' Federation Eurovélo 4 route (Roscoff to Kiev) is the same route as the V4 La Littorale, which is further overlaid by the Tour de Manche, a cross-channel, circular route through Brittany, part of Normandy and southern England.

The V1 is not described in this book except from Roscoff to Port de Carhaix, where it is the same route as the V7. From Port de Carhaix it follows the Nantes-Brest canal, which is fully described in *The Nantes-Brest Canal - a guide for walkers and cyclists* by Wendy Mewes (Red Dog Books). Also the V4 and V5 La Littorale (the coastal routes) are not described here because new sections are regularly being added, and very little is actually on Green Way.

The V8 St-Brieuc to Lorient,however, is now practicable from near St-Brieuc to Hennebont, not far from Lorient, and the central Green Way section along the Rigole d'Hilvern is now part of this guide.

In addition to the long-distance cycle routes using Green Ways there are other shorter Green Ways that have been developed independently of any immediate overall route plan. The old railway line from Quimper to Douarnenez, for example, starting where it branched from the still functioning line to Châteaulin, is a particularly attractive Green Way of some 18 kilometres. (See p.15 for a list of Green Ways in Brittany.)

Green Way from Guengat (Quimper) to Douarnenez

ENGINEERING

Although co-ordinated from Rennes, the actual work of development and maintenance of the Green Ways is carried out by the departments and this leads to variations in surface, signage, and the safety of road crossings.

An overlapping barrier across the Green Way certainly prevents any motorised traffic from wandering onto the Green Way, and also prevents an unwary cyclist from speeding across a road without looking, but if the overlapping elements are set too close together they become a serious obstacle for cyclists, especially those encumbered with panniers or trailers. In other places this seems to have been recognised and there are no barriers at all, the presence of the road being marked by a sort of 'wiggle' in the Green Way and a 'Stop' sign.

The most common surface is a sort of macadam without the tar but with a top dressing of fine gravelly sand, rolled hard. This is good for cycling but can become grassed over where traffic is light or where it isn't regularly maintained. It can also suffer from flood damage if the drainage is not properly engineered, making a bumpy ride for cyclists. In Morbihan the V3 Green Way from Mauron to Questembert is tarmac and in good condition, which brings the roller-bladers out in force on a Sunday afternoon. In general, canal towpaths which have been in use a lot longer than the converted railways are often tarmac but in poor condition.

USAGE

Green Ways are open to everyone except motorised traffic, provided the surface is suitable. Horse riders, where allowed, are subject to some restrictions - usually to keep to a walk and use the middle of the track. Roller-bladers will want to seek out the tarmac sections for a smooth roll. Electric bikes are permitted and in some areas seem quite popular. Electric wheel-chairs, too, should not have any problems on better maintained Green Ways.

All of Brittany's Green Ways are suitable for mountain bikes (VTT) and hybrid bikes (VTC). Some are suitable as well for road bikes and racing bikes but if undertaking a tour of Brittany's Green Ways it would probably be inadvisable to choose a racing or road bike, the best option being a hybrid or a mountain bike. With a mountain bike you have a greater choice of detours away from the Green Way and can take advantage of some of the excellent VTT circuits of varying difficulty that depart from the Green Way.

Travelling the Green Ways of Brittany is a very pleasant and enriching experience. Passing through deep countryside, often far from roads or habitation, wildlife is ever present and the scenery can be spectacular. Frequently a short detour will reveal a surprising feature of Brittany's rich heritage and there are many possible cycle tours or walking circuits deviating from the Green Way for a few kilometres to discover the surrounding area.

Over long distances, away from towns and off season the Green Ways are usually deserted, but at other times one is likely to encounter all types of Green Way users - from cyclists, joggers, serious long-distance runners, roller-bladers and uni-cyclists to *monsieur et madame* out for a stroll with their dog.

GLOSSARY

abri	shelter
balade	a walk, a stroll
balade vélo	a bike ride
bois	woods
bourg	village/small town with shops, bar, etc.
chemin	way, track, very minor road
Chouan	Breton, catholic counter-revolutionary
clocher	church tower
écluse	lock
enclos paroissial	parish enclosure (a church-yard with certain specific architectural features)
gare	station
hôtel	besides the obvious, can also mean a large town house
hypermarché	large supermarket with ancillary shops and services
itinéraire	route
landes	heathland
location	hire (*location de vélos* = bicycle hire)
randonnée	a walk, a ride or a drive (for leisure)
route	road
vélo	bicycle
véloroute	cycle route
voie ferrée	railway
voie verte	Green Way

ABBREVIATIONS

GR	*Grand Randonnée* - long distance footpath, designated by the FFRP (Federation Francaise de la Randonnée Pédestre). GR waymarks are white over red.
GRP	*Grand Randonnée de Pays* - long distance circuit to discover a particular region.
TER	*Trains Express Régionaux* (regional express trains) - regional here means Brittany, a 'region' of France. (TER trains carry bicycles free, provided there is room.)
VTC	*vélo tout chemin* - hybrid bike.
VTT	*vélo tout terrain* - mountain bike.

ABOUT THIS BOOK

This is a guide mainly for cyclists in Brittany, whether cycling through Brittany en route for the rest of France, or travelling around within Brittany, enjoying what it has to offer. It is also for occasional cyclists - those touring by car or camper van, with a couple of bikes on the back to take advantage of any cycling opportunity that presents itself. Walkers and anyone else who enjoys the open air will also find it useful.

The book is divided into four parts:

1. The List (see page 15). A list of cycle routes using Green Ways and some other useful cycle routes. Together with the map, repeated inside the front cover, this gives a reasonably complete picture of the Green Ways and signed cycle routes at the time of writing.

2. Railways (see page 25). Many of the Green Ways have been shaped by the engineering needs of now defunct railways. To aid casual tourists and ardent railway fans alike to identify with the routes they are travelling, this chapter on Brittany's railway history is accompanied by a schematic map showing past as well as present railways.

3. The described routes. The core of the book is a guide to the network of cycle routes using Green Ways that make it possible to travel long distances across Brittany, away from motorised traffic.

4. Accommodation. At the back of the book, where it is easy to find, is the list of accommodation, intended to be used in conjunction with the maps of the described routes. It's therefore arranged in the same short geographical sections as those routes.

THE DESCRIBED ROUTES

Of course you can follow Green Ways in either direction but for simplicity they are described here in the same sense as they are named. Thus for the **V7 Roscoff to Concarneau**, Section 1 starts at Roscoff and the last section, Section 12, ends a few kilometres short of Concarneau. Coincidentally, or maybe not, this system is tailor-made for anyone starting at the ferry terminals of Roscoff or St-Malo.

At first glance the amount of information on each page may appear daunting but it is presented in a consistent way so that the reader will soon become familiar with the lay-out and be able to pick out the information required at any moment.

The key elements are:
- **map**
- **gradient profile**
- **basic route information** - signage - route - surface - difficulties - detours
- **Liaisons** - links with other routes, circuits and public transport
- **Places of interest nearby**
- **Refreshments** and **Provisions**

The map shows
- the route of the Green Way or cycle route
- road and track crossings
- the surrounding road system
- car parks with easy access to the Green Way
- where other cycling or walking routes or circuits **leave** the Green Way (liaisons)
- the approximate location of overnight accommodation
- places mentioned in the text and 'places of interest nearby'.
- also shown are places where you can sit down, have a picnic, or shelter from the rain (often quite difficult in the middle of nowhere).

For the list of Map Symbols see page 12.

Gradient Profile is based on a GPS trace, normally from Point A to Point B on the nearby map.

Basic route information

Signage Green Ways are not hard to follow as long as you know where they are going. Under the heading 'Signage' is a sequential list of places that are likely to show on route signs, according to your direction of travel (▶S = direction south, ▶N = direction north, etc.)

Route This will usually just give an idea of the nature of the Green Way or cycle route (former railway or canal towpath, for example). Where more detailed instructions about how to follow the route are required, they will be given here.

Surface The surface of Green Ways varies depending on the authority through whose jurisdiction it passes. Some have chosen to cover it with tarmac, while most are content with compacted sand. The condition of these surfaces can vary from new to worn-out and overgrown. A note of the surface is given for each section, together with an idea of its condition (at the time of writing) using the following terms:

good = new and/or well maintained, no problems encountered;

fair = no major problems but perhaps showing signs of wear;

poor = worn out, pot-holes, or tarmac surface breaking up, or sand surface overgrown and/or muddy or flood damaged).

Difficulties There are very few difficulties and nobody has set out to put difficulties in your way - quite the reverse, but occasionally minor obstacles get overlooked, or a planned improvement has not yet been carried out. Where such things have been noticed they are included in the basic route information.

Detours These are usually suggestions for minor diversions you can take to find something interesting. Occasionally there will be a suggestion for a longer digression from the Green Way, but normally the longer tours are recognised circuits and thus featured under 'Liaisons'.

Liaisons

Many local circuits, either walking, cycling, or mountain biking (VTT), cross over the Green Ways or follow them for some distance. The points where these routes <u>depart</u> from the Green Way are marked on the maps with an appropriate symbol and a number or letter cross-referenced to the nearby list of liaisons.

The direction of circuits, clockwise or anti-clockwise, is shown with a symbol thus: ↻.or ↺, ◉ or ◉. Usually, mountain bike and cycling circuits are graded for difficulty, often by a colour code: for an explanation of the grades see p.13.

If these circuits are known locally by any particular name or number, that will be used, to help you identify it in any tourist literature or on wayside signs.

If there is no local number, it is given a letter or number for cross-referencing between the map and the list of liaisons.

Where possible, a convenient starting point for circuits, with parking, will be suggested for anyone not arriving via the Green Way.

Other liaisons are links with any public transport which can accept bicycles (so buses are not included). TER (*trains express régionaux*) is the regional train service that carries your bicycle free as long as there is room for it. Under liaisons the name of the station on the map is given first, followed by possible destinations. (See also the railway map on p.25, and www.ter-sncf.com)

Places of interest nearby

These include the sort of places that you might regret having missed through not knowing you were so near them.

Refreshments and Provisions

Long stretches of the Green Way routes pass through deep countryside where population is sparse and there are no shops, bars, cafés or restaurants. It's therefore quite important to know where your next meal is coming from. Under this heading are listed the towns or villages that have shops and usually at least a bar as well. Where a wayside café or restaurant has been noticed in passing it will be marked on the map and noted under this heading. This is not a recommendation - just telling you it was there at the time of writing. Bear in mind that shops close between noon and 2.00, and sometimes 3.00 if they are staying open into the evening. Their opening times are in tune with the local pace of life - you just need to adjust. It's a good idea to carry some basic rations with you, even if you never have to use them.

MAP SYMBOLS

▆▆▆▆	Green Way (no motorised traffic, easy gradients, prepared surface)
▆▆▆	Green Way route continued and signed on roads shared with motorised traffic
•••••••	Suggested alternative to signed route
▭▭▭	Green Way route continued, but not signed, on roads shared with motorised traffic (un-signed, so only suggested)
● ● ● ●	Green Way route, practicable but not yet developed to full Green Way standard (possible lack of signs, poor surface, unsecured junctions, etc.)
‒‒▭▭▭	detour route
✕	minor road or track crossing
✖	busy road crossing
┼┼┼┼✖	railway/level crossing
▬▬▬▪	canal/lock
P	parking
WC	toilets
⍩	water
✖	picnic table/area
⋀⋀	seat
⋔	shelter (often a trackside hut, somewhere to get out of the rain)
✕	restaurant
⑤	supermarket
TO▶	position of Tourist Office
i	tourist information point
Ⓜ	museum
⊡	sports field
▣	racecourse (*hippodrome*)
⚐	abbey
⛪	church (usually the centre of a *bourg*)
+	chapel
⊞	cemetery

Departments of Brittany (and their number):

Côtes d'Armor (22)
Finistère (29)
Ille-et-Vilaine (35)
Loire-Atlantique (44)
Morbihan (56)

liaisons

V4	Green Way
VD **VD6**	departmental cycle routes
⊙	cycle tour/circuit clockwise
⊙	cycle tour/circuit anti-clockwise
⊙	cycle tour/circuit, direction not specified
6	VTT (mountain bike) circuit
a	walking circuit
GR380	GR - *grande randonnée* - long-distance footpath
🚆	train service TER (bikes accepted)
⛴	ferry/boat service

accommodation

4*	hotel/B&B/chambre d'hôte
6	gîte d'étape/hostel
2	camping

GRADING OF CYCLE TOURS

easy = fairly level, roads and/or well-maintained tracks
medium = some hills and possibly earth tracks
energetic = very up and down (possibility of poor surfaces at the limit of VTC capability)

In some places a colour-coded four grade system is used, similar to the standardised VTT grades (below).

GRADING OF VTT/MOUNTAIN BIKE ROUTES - COLOUR-CODED:

green = family (*famille*)
blue = leisure, easy (*loisir, facile*)
red = sport, difficult (*sportif, difficile*)
black = extreme, very difficult (*extrème, très difficile*)

SIGNS

Generally, cycle routes are well signed, although circuits are often signed in one direction only. On the few occasions when there appears to be a lack of signs, the rule that usually holds good is to follow the road you are on. (This also applies where there is a sign but it doesn't clearly indicate any direction.)

Occasionally a signed route will vary from the published one. This might be the result of problems occurring after the route has been published, so in these circumstances it is best to follow the signs rather than the book.

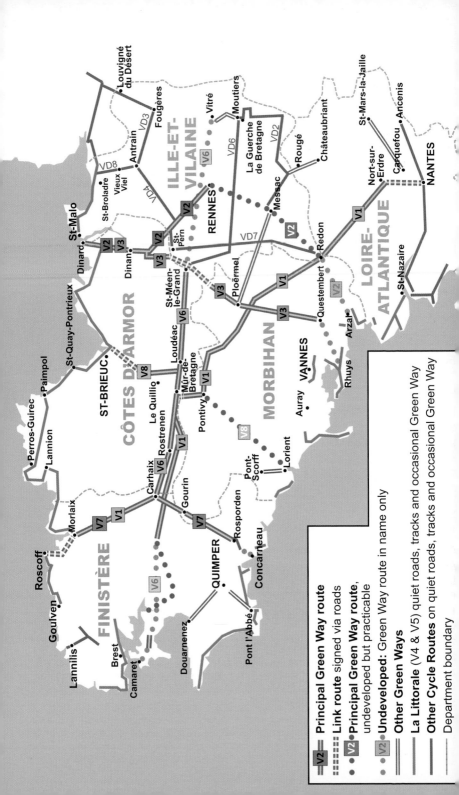

Louvigné
du Désert

Vitré

Moutiers

Fougères

VD3

Antrain

ILLE-ET-
VILAINE

VD6

Châteaubriant

VD2

Rougé

St-Mars-la-Jaille

Ancenis

Carquefou

VD8

Vieux
Viel

St-Brolade

La Guerche
de Bretagne

Messac

Nort-sur-
Erdre

NANTES

St-Malo

VD4

V2

RENNES

V1

LOIRE-
ATLANTIQUE

St-Nazaire

Dinard

V2

V3

V2

St-
Pern

VD7

V2

Redon

V2

Paimpol

Dinan

V3

V3

Ploërmel

Questembert

Arzal

St-Quay-Pontrieux

St-Méen-
le-Grand

V6

V3

V1

V3

Perros-Guirec

CÔTES D'ARMOR

Loudéac

V1

VANNES

Lannion

ST-BRIEUC

V8

Mûr-de-
Bretagne

V1

MORBIHAN

Rhuys

Le Quillio

Rostrenen

Pontivy

Auray

Morlaix

V7

V1

Carhaix

V6

V1

Gourin

V7

V8

Pont-
Scorff

Lorient

Roscoff

Goulven

Rosporden

Lannilis

FINISTÈRE

V6

Brest

QUIMPER

Concarneau

Camaret

Douarnenez

Pont l'Abbé

V2 **Principal Green Way route**

Link route signed via roads

V2 **Principal Green Way route,** undeveloped but practicable

V2 **Undeveloped:** Green Way route in name only

Other Green Ways

La Littorale (V4 & V5) quiet roads, tracks and occasional Green Way

Other Cycle Routes on quiet roads, tracks and occasional Green Way

Department boundary

Green Ways & Cycle Routes

Green Ways and cycle routes in Brittany are in a process of on-going development. The information given here reflects their state in the latter half of 2013, according to information available at that time.

NB - To avoid any unnecessary confusion, the names of cycle routes and Green Ways used here conform to those used officially and in other tourist literature. These names tend to express a long-term plan rather than a present reality, so be sure to read the small print.

REGIONAL ROUTES

Name: **V1 Roscoff to Nantes** (part of **Velodyssey*** from Ilfracombe in Devon to Hendaye on the French/Spanish border)

Developed: Roscoff to Nantes

Length: 358kms (approximately)

Type: cycle route, largely on Green Way (canal towpath or railway)

Route: Roscoff - St-Pol-de-Léon - Morlaix - Poullaouen - Carhaix - (Port de Carhaix) - Rostrenen - Gouarec - Lac de Guerlédan - Pontivy - Rohan - Josselin - Malestroit - Redon - Guenrouët - Blain - Nort-sur-Erdre - Nantes.

Starts at Roscoff and shares the V7 cycle-route (see below) to Morlaix then the V7 Green Way to Carhaix. From here to Gouarec there is a choice of routes.

Alternative 1 (shorter): follow the V6 from Carhaix to Gouarec.

Alternative 2 (prettier): from Carhaix, continue on the V7 to Port de Carhaix (or just before at the bridge over the canal, see map on p.107) then follow the canal towpath eastward to Gouarec.

From Gouarec the V1 is contiguous with the V6 to a point just east of Lac de Guerlédan, where the V1 leaves southwards on a signed linking route to rejoin the Nantes-Brest Canal (below the barrage de Guerlédan), and follow it to Pontivy. From Pontivy the V1 continues eastwards on the canal. Just before the end of the canal the V1 (signed as Velodyssey) diverts southwards to re-integrate with the road system to Nantes (c.25kms including some further sections of Green Way or cycle track).

*Velodyssey is part of the EuroVelo Atlantic Coast route (Ev1) from the North Cape in Norway to Sagres in Portugal (Eurovelo is a concept of the European Cyclists' Federation, www.ecf.com).

Name: **V2 St-Malo to Arzal**
Developed: St-Malo - Rennes
Length: 107kms (including 4kms by ferry across the Rance)
Type: mostly Green Way (railway or towpath)
Route: St-Malo - (ferry across the Rance) - Dinard - Pleslin-Trigavou
             - St-Samson-sur-Rance - Dinan - Léhon - Evran - Tinténiac -
             Hédé - Rennes

(Rennes to Redon along the river Vilaine towpath is not yet fully
developed as a Green Way but is practicable. Redon to Arzal is not yet
developed so cannot be relied upon)

If you don't wish to visit St-Malo, it makes little difference to start at Dinard.
From the old station at Dinard the V2 follows the former railway south, passing
Dinard Airport and Pleslin-Trigavou, continuing through Tréméreuc (link to V4
Littoral) to St-Samson-sur-Rance. Here the V2 follows minor roads through
Taden to the banks of the Rance, there to follow the towpath to Port de Dinan.
From Dinan a temporary section continues on the left bank of the Rance to
Léhon. From Léhon the V2 follows the towpath of the Ille-et-Rance canal
through Hédé (link to St-Pern, near Plouasne on the V3) and Montreuil-sur-
Ille (link to Antrain) then all the way to Rennes. After Rennes the Green Way
is still to be developed, but it is possible to follow the Vilaine all the way,
through Messac (link to Ploërmel) to Redon (link to V1 and the Nantes-Brest
Canal).

Name: **V3 St-Malo to Rhuys** (Presqu'île de Rhuys, Gulf of
             Morbihan).
Developed: St-Malo - Questembert
Length: 113kms (including 4kms by ferry across the Rance)
Type: mostly Green Way (railway or towpath), 39kms of shared
             road between Médréac and Mauron
Route: St-Malo - (ferry across the Rance) - Dinard - Pleslin-Trigavou
             - St-Samson-sur-Rance - Dinan - Léhon - Trévron - Le Quiou -
             Plouasne - Médréac - St-Méen-le-Grand - Gaël - St-Léry -
             Mauron - Loyat - Ploërmel - Malestroit - Questembert

(the continuation to Presqu'île de Rhuys is not yet developed)

The V3 duplicates the V2 from St-Malo to the Écluse du Mottay, south of
Léhon. Here the V3 leaves the canal to strike across country by road to Trévron
to pick up a former railway, which it follows southwards past Le Quiou and
Plouasne (nearby link to Hédé, on the V2). Just before Médréac the Green Way
stops at the D220. There follows a section of about 39kms by roads, through
St-Méen-le-Grand (link with V6 to Carhaix) to St-Léry. From there a short
section of Green Way reaches the outskirts of Mauron in the department of
Morbihan. Now a Green Way again, this time with tarmac, it picks up the
former railway from Mauron. The Lac au Duc (lake) is on the right just before

the next important town, Ploërmel (link to Messac on the Vilaine to the east). Continuing south the V3 crosses the Nantes-Brest canal (link to V1) three times before reaching the outskirts of Malestroit and continuing on over the Landes de Lanvaux (a long, low range of hills covered mostly by heathland - *landes*). The Green Way ends at Bel Air, about 3kms short of Questembert.

Name: **V4 and V5 La Littorale**

Developed: piece-meal

Length: potentially, several hundred kilometres - now almost half of it developed as a cycle route

Type: cycle-route on shared roads and farm tracks with just a few short sections of Green Way

Route: Following approximately the coastline of Brittany. The **V4** runs from the Normandy border to Roscoff, the **V5** covers the rest of the Brittany coast.

This project had a major boost in 2013 from the inauguration of the **Tour de Manche** linking the Devon and Dorset coast with the north Brittany coast and the Cotentin peninsula in Normandy.

La Littorale currently consists of:

• a more or less continuous signed route from the Normandy border to Goulven on the north Finistère coast, west of Roscoff

• Lampaul-Plouarzel to Le Conquet

• Le Conquet to Brest and up the river Élorn to La Forêt Landerneau

• a section from the Pointe du Raz to St-Guénolé, then Penmarch to Loctudy.

• a shared road route from Pont l'Abbé to La Forêt-Fouesnant, with two surfaced Green Way spurs towards the coast.

• a shared route from Trégunc to Trévignon

• Guidel Plages to Kerroch on surfaced Green Way

• some Green Way sections around Erdeven and the Quiberon peninsular and part of a route from Erdeven inland to Auray

• a short section of surfaced Green Way near Le Bono

• from 3kms northeast of Aradon, passing south of Vannes to Theix - on the Presqu'île de Rhuys (initially on surfaced Green Way)

• Presqu'île de Rhuys from north-east of St-Armel to Port Navalo, with a spur from Sarzeau eastwards to Le Tour du Parc.

• from Ferel to Pénestin to the border of Morbihan and Loire Atlantique, then a section from Mesquer to St-Molf

• in Loire Atlantique its continuation is known as Vélocéan, starting at Piriac-sur-Mer (see below).

Name:	**V6 Camaret to Vitré**
Developed:	Pont Triffen to St-Méen-Le-Grand
Length:	147kms
Type:	Green Way (only a few short stretches of shared road)
Route:	Pont Triffen - Port de Carhaix - then via V7 north to Carhaix - Maël-Carhaix - Rostrenen - Gouarec - Bon Repos - Caurel - Mûr de Bretagne - St-Guen - St-Caradec - Loudéac - Plémet - Laurenan - Merdrignac - Trémorel - St-Méen-le-Grand

Although named "Camaret to Vitré" the V6 is complete only in its central section from Pont Triffen to St-Méen-le-Grand.

A section of former railway running parallel with the Nantes-Brest Canal from Pont Triffen to Port de Carhaix has been recently developed to Green Way standard, effectively extending the V6 westwards from Carhaix to Pont Triffen. From Pont Triffen westwards the towpath of the Nantes-Brest Canal provides a continuation to Châteaulin (level but with many loops so longer than any road route). From Châteaulin to Camaret nothing is yet developed, except a 4km section of Green Way from Tal-ar-Groas to Crozon.

In the east, the V6 is undeveloped between St-Méen-le-Grand and Vitré (but see Ille-et-Vilaine cycle route VD6, p.22).

Name:	**V7 Roscoff to Concarneau**
Developed:	Roscoff to La Boissière, Concarneau
Length:	136kms (Roscoff to La Boissière)
Type:	Roscoff to Morlaix is a cycle route Morlaix to Rosporden is mostly Green Way
Route:	Roscoff - St-Pol-de-Léon - Lanvéguen - Penzé - Morlaix - Poullaouen - Carhaix - Port de Carhaix - Gourin - Guiscriff - Scaër - Rosporden - Concarneau

From Roscoff the route is signed mostly on minor roads to Morlaix. The Green Way starts at Morlaix, on the track-bed of the old Réseau Breton, soon climbing steadily to the highest point over the Monts d'Arrée at Kermeur. From here there is some exceptional scenery through wooded valleys with fast flowing rivers to Poullaouen and on to Carhaix. Through Carhaix the road route is fairly well signed and soon picks up the Green Way following the railway again down to Port de Carhaix on the Nantes-Brest Canal. Another high spot over the Black Mountains then an easy ride through Gourin, Guiscriff and Scaër to Rosporden. Here the Green Way ends and there is a signed continuation of the route as far as La Boissière just south of the N165.

Name:	**V8 St-Brieuc to Lorient**
Developed:	developed from Yffiniac (near St-Brieuc) to Pontivy, practicable from Pontivy to Hennebont
Length:	c.150kms Yffiniac to Hennebont
Type:	mixed Green Way and shared roads
Route:	Yffiniac (link with V4 La Littorale) - Barrage de Bosméléac - via Rigole d'Hilvern to St Caradec - via V6 to Mûr-de-Bretagne - via V1 to Pontivy - via Blavet canal towpath to Hennebont

Development of the Rigole d'Hilvern already continues beyond the V6 as far as Hémonstoir. Were it to carry on to the Nantes-Brest Canal at Hilvern it would offer an alternative route to Pontivy, approaching from the east along the canal.

Rigole d'Hilvern

Name:	**Ploërmel - Messac**
	(signed as VD6 in Morbihan, VD2 in Ille-et-Vilaine)
Developed:	All the way
Length:	47kms
Type:	Green Way (former railway)
Route:	Ploërmel (link to V3) - Guer - Maure de Bretagne - Guipry - Messac

Links the V3 at Ploërmel with the V2's undeveloped route on the Vilaine at Messac.

OTHER GREEN WAYS AND CYCLE ROUTES by department.

VD (*Véloroute Départementale*) cycle routes are numbered by the department. Thus the VD6 in Morbihan is **not** the same route as the VD6 in Ille-et-Vilaine (although they are near enough to cause confusion).

FINISTÈRE

Name:	**Chemin de randonnée de Guengat à Douarnenez**
Length:	18kms
Type:	Green Way
Route:	Ty-Planche - Guengat - Plogonnec - Le Juch - Douarnenez - Tréboul

Starts at Ty Planche on the D63, 6km northwest of Quimper. Follows a former railway track-bed all the way to Douarnenez. Passes close to Locronan - '*Petite Cité de Caractère*' and one of the 'most beautiful villages of France' (accessible from Le Juch) - then arrives in Douarnenez opposite Port Rhu. To visit the Boat Museum in Port Rhu (recommended) turn right from the Green Way at the main road where a Total filling station is to the left, after 50m fork left, following signs to *Le Port*. For the leisure port of Tréboul and Île Tristan continue to the end of the Green Way, bear right and follow signs.

Name:	**Chemin de randonnée de Pluguffan à Pont-l'Abbé**
Length:	12kms
Type:	Green Way
Route:	(through the communes of) Pluguffan - Plomelin - Combrit - Tréméoc - Plonéour-Lanvern - Pont-l'Abbé. (Links to V5 La Littorale go east from the southern part of this Green Way)

Starts about 7km southwest of central Quimper, at the roundabout on the D56, north side of the D785 intersection. There is a small car park with an almost hidden entrance directly off the roundabout. From the end of the car park follow signs to 'Pont l'Abbé *via voie ferrée*'. If starting from Pont l'Abbé follow signs to *la gare* (north of the river). Facing the old station building (now the *Maison des Associations*) follow the road to your right. Where it bears left and crosses the line of the old railway there is a small car park on the left and the Green Way starts on the right.

Name:	**Véloroute des Abers**
Length:	40kms
Type:	cycle route
Route:	Aber Wrac'h - Lannilis - Plouvien - Plabennec - then dividing, south to Gouesnou, north to Le Drennec

There are plans to extend the northern branch to Lesneven. The southern branch could also be extended from Gouesnou to Brest in the years to come.

Some busses in Finistère carry bicycles during the summer.
For details see www.viaoo29.fr

Name: **Lorient to Pont-Scorff**

Length: 6kms

Type: Green Way (railway)

Route: Quéven - Pont-Scorff Zoo - Pont-Scorff.
               (This Green Way is part of Morbihan's VD1 which will
               eventually link Lorient to Gourin via Plouay and Le Faouët.)

Starts at Quéven, 5km northwest of the centre of Lorient (there is a cycle path from central Lorient). From Quéven church go north-east on rue de la Gare for 200m to find the Green Way on the left, opposite the École Anatole France. There follows 6km of Green Way along the former railway Lorient - Pont Scorff, crossing the river Scarve by a viaduct and passing Pont Scorff Zoo. It arrives at the western outskirts of Pont-Scorff where newer roads become superimposed on the line of the old railway. One can follow ahead on *rue* F. Mauriac, then on *rue du* Dr. Rialland to find a continuation of the Green Way for another 600m.

    Pont-Scorff is an interesting small town noted for its many art and craft workshops.

ILLE-ET-VILAINE

Name: **VD2 Guer** (Morbihan) **- Moutiers**

Length: approx. 120kms

Type: Green Way from Guer to Messac and from Bains-de-Bretagne
               to east of Teillay, otherwise cycle route

Route: Guer - Maure-de-Bretagne - Messac - Bain-de-Bretagne - Teillay
               - Martigné-Ferchaud - La Guerche-de-Bretagne - Moutiers

The VD2 is an extension of the Ploërmel to Messac Green Way (see p. 19), which has been following a railway line that once ran from Ploërmel to Châteaubriant (see page 25). Just east of Teillay the VD2 leaves this line and finds its way to Moutiers, where it joins the VD6 (see page 22).

Name: **VD3 / VD8 Fougères - St-Broladre**

Length: 61kms

Type: Fougères to Antrain mostly Green Way, cycle route from
               Antrain to Roz-sur-Couesnon, then Green Way to St-Broladre

Route: Fougères - St-Germain-en-Coglès - St-Etienne-en-Coglès -
               St-Brice-en-Coglès - Antrain - Sougéal - Vieux-Viel

The Green Way VD3 from Fougères to Antrain follows a former railway from the centre of Fougères. At the midway point the Green Way is diverted alongside a road for a kilometre to near St-Etienne-du-Coglès. The last few kilometres approaching Antrain are said to be the quietest and prettiest, passing through a wooded river valley, with a short tunnel. From Antrain the VD3 continues as a cycle route to Vieux-Viel, from where it continues as the VD8. At les Quatre Salines, a hamlet in the lowlands between St-Broladre and Roz-sur-Couesnon, the VD8 meets the V4 Littorale coming from Normandy and shares its Green Way to the Chapelle Ste-Anne (Bay of Mont St-Michel).

Name: **VD4 St-Pern - Antrain**
Length: 70kms
Type: cycle route
Route: St-Pern - Miniac-sous-Bécherel - Cardroc - Les Iffs -
            St-Brieuc-des-Iffs - Hédé - Montreuil-sur-Ille - Feins -
            Marcillé-Raoul - Bazouges-la-Pérouse - Antrain.

At St-Pern, the V3 is only 2kms away at Plouasne, over the border in Morbihan (see p.53 for liaison). The route goes from St-Pern via Miniac-sous-Bécherel (but don't miss nearby Bécherel, Brittany's equivalent of Hay-on-Wye for bookshops). Then on through Les Iffs, where a detour is in order to the Château Montmuran (see page 45). Continuing via St-Brieuc-des-Iffs to Hédé and the Ille-et-Rance canal (V2 Green Way). Leaving the canal again at Montreuil-sur-Ille the route continues via Feins, Marcillé-Raoul and Bazouges-la-Pérouse to Antrain.

Name: **VD5 Fougères - Louvigné-du-Désert**
Length: 22kms
Type: Green Way (railway)
Route: Fougères - St-Germain-en-Coglès - Le Châtellier - Parigné -
            Louvigné-du-Désert

Starts near centre of Fougères, from the parking du Nançon, initially following the same route as VD3 (see p.21). After 4.5kms, at a crossing 1km after the D782, the line forks. Divert a few metres right to take the right hand track (straight on goes to Antrain). After Louvigné-du-Désert the Green Way continues towards St-Hilaire du Harcouët in Normandy (Manche) and on to the Green Way east/west from Vire to the Bay of Mont St-Michel (V4).

Name: **VD6 St-Méen-le-Grand to Vitré**
Length: approx. 135kms
Type: cycle route St-Méen-le-Grand to Moutiers;
            Green Way (railway) Moutiers to Vitré
Route: St-Méen-le-Grand - St-Malon-sur-Mel - Plélan-le-Grand -
            Bréal-sous-Montfort - Le Pont Réan (on the River Vilaine) -
            Pont Péan - Amanlis - Essé - Marcillé Robert - Moutiers -
            Vitré

From St-Malon-sur-Mel to Plélan-le-Grand the route passes through the legendary Forest of Brocéliande. Later, between Essé and Marcillé Robert, don't miss the massive dolmen 'La Roche aux Fées' beside the D341.

Roche aux Fées

Name: **VD7 St-Pern to Redon**
Length: approx 110kms
Type: cycle route
Route: St-Pern (link to VD4) - Iffendic - Monterfil - Maxent - Pipriac
- St-Just - Redon (link to Nantes-Brest Canal V1)

In conjunction with the VD4, this is a useful north-south route linking the V3 Green Way at Plouasne or the V2 at Hédé with the V1 Nantes-Brest Canal (Velodyssey) at Redon. Highlight on the way for megalith hunters is the megalithic site at St-Just, second only to Carnac.

Name: **VD8 Vieux-Viel - St-Broladre**
(see VD3 / VD8 Fougères to St-Broladre, page 21)

<u>LOIRE ATLANTIQUE</u>

Name: **Vélocéan** (north of Loire)
Length: 46kms
Type: cycle route on roads
Route: Piriac-sur-Mer - Guérande - branch to Le Croisic - La Baule -
St-Nazaire

Piriac-sur-Mer (*Petite Cité de Caractère*) is a seaside resort with a marina. Guérande, a well-preserved medieval walled town gave its name to the Treaty of Guérande (1364) that ended Brittany's War of Succession. For more than a thousand years salt has been produced from the extensive salt marshes in the area. The route branches to Le Croisic, seaside town on a peninsula beyond the salt marshes, La Baule,

Salt marsh near Guérande

resort with extensive harbour, leisure port and plenty of restaurants, and St-Nazaire, industrial town, port and dockyard.

The extensive wetland area of the Parc Naturel Régional de Brière and the Château de Ranrouët at Herbignac could make an interesting detour inland.

Name: **Vélocéan** (south of Loire)
Length: 39kms
Type: cycle route
Route: St-Brévin - St-Michel-Chef-Chef - branch to Préfailles - Pornic
- Les Moutiers-en-Retz

Although the route follows minor roads and non-motorised trackways, main road crossings can be difficult in summer when traffic is heavy.

Bridge over the Loire, St-Nazaire

Name: **La Loire à Vélo en Loire-Atlantique**
          (also known as Eurovélo La Loire or Eurovéloroute No.6)
Length: 88kms (estimated)
Type: cycle route, variable: earth path to city cycle lanes to shared
          roads to quasi-Green Way
Route: St-Brévin - Paimboeuf - Le Pellerin - Couëron - Nantes -
          Mauves-sur-Loire - Oudon - Ancenis

On the south bank of the mouth of the Loire from St-Brévin to Le Pellerin.
On the north bank from Couëron, through Nantes to Mauves-sur-Loire, Oudon and
Ancenis

Name: **Carquefou - St-Mars-la-Jaille**
Length: 36kms
Type: Green Way (railway)
Route: Carquefou - St-Mars-du-Désert - Ligné - Teillé - Pannecé -
          St Mars-la-Jaille

Starts at Carquefou on the north eastern outskirts of Nantes and goes to
St-Mars-la-Jaille on the border with Maine-et-Loire. From Carquefou church
go north on Rue François-René de Chateaubriand for 800m. At roundabout
turn right on Rue d'Atalante to find Green Way on left after 50m. Earlier reports
of this Green Way mention dangerous road crossings with no signs to slow
traffic: this may have been rectified more recently but be cautious.

Name: **Châteaubriant - Rougé**
Length: 12kms
Type: Green Way (railway)
Route: Châteaubriant - Ruffigné - Rougé

A well-signed, well-surfaced (tarmac) Green Way on a former railway. Starts
1.7kms from centre of Châteaubriant: from the church go west on bvd.de la
République (to St-Aubin-des-Châteaux), continue ahead on Avenue des
Anciens Combattants, then at Hyper-U roundabout turn left on Ave. Pierre
Mendès-France, then right on Ave. de la Citoyenneté, which leads up to the
start of the Green Way. After Rougé the last 2kms to the Loire Atlantique
border are not tarmac. Over the border it joins the Ille et Vilaine cycle route
VD6 (see page 22).

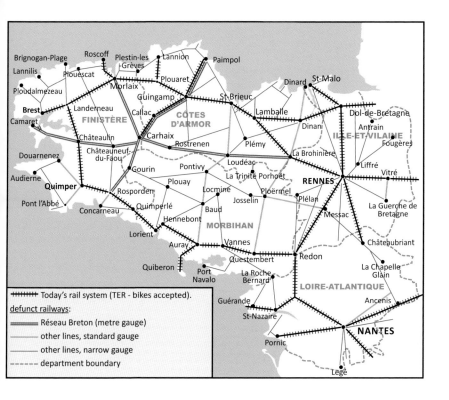

Today's rail system (TER - bikes accepted).

defunct railways:
Réseau Breton (metre gauge)
other lines, standard gauge
other lines, narrow gauge
department boundary

THE RAILWAYS IN BRITTANY

Overview

Hard on the heels of the early 19th century development of a canal network in Brittany came a competitive newcomer in the form of the railway. The Second Empire was a time of progress in France, with Napoléon III (who was to visit Brittany himself in 1858) a keen proponent of the railway – but because of the extreme westerly position of the region, trains arrived on Breton soil rather later than in many other parts of France. One important service they provided early on was to bring Breton granite blocks to Paris for the grandiose re-development schemes of Baron Hussmann.

The system began in Nantes, then a part of the region, in 1851. Initially a central main line via Rennes-Pontivy-Châteaulin-Brest was envisaged, but this idea was abandoned on the grounds that it replicated the route of the Nantes-Best canal. The accepted alternative was separate northern and southern routes.

In 1857 Rennes station was functioning, and over the next ten years the main line routes were gradually created. The northern route to Brest passed through St-Brieuc and Morlaix, and in the south trains from Nantes reached Quimper via Vannes and Lorient. In the centre of Brittany the Réseau Breton, a narrow gauge system, fanned out in a star shape from Carhaix to reach coastal towns like Paimpol on the north coast and Camaret on the Atlantic edge of the Crozon peninsula. Other secondary lines were later built in all departments. It is the former track beds of these metre gauge routes that now provide the bulk of the Green Ways for leisure use.

The impetus for the elaboration of this system was both the transport of goods and also passenger facilities. Where schedules were related to town market days and places of employment, demand was assured, but numbers of regular users on the smaller lines never reached levels of long-term economic viability. Movement of freight by rail had greater success initially, but as the quality of road transport progressed rapidly in the 20th century, it was to prove finally an unequal competition.

Creation of the railways

The development of the railways was a state-organised and partly state-funded project with individual areas leased to companies who would construct the lines and related buildings, procure locomotives and employ the workers needed to keep the system functioning. Firstly feasibility studies were needed to sort out the routes, and these were usually decided on the basis of geography and gradient, given Brittany's hilly landscape, rather than in response to the clamouring of local communities hoping to bring this new-fangled opportunity for economic development to their areas.

All this construction provided much needed employment, particularly in the rural areas of central Brittany. Once routes had been agreed and land bought – voluntarily offered or through compulsory purchase – the elaborate work of creating the track-beds, with all the concomitant labour of clearing trees, forming embankments, cuttings and run-off channels for water, and the building of tunnels, bridges, viaducts and stations could begin.

The workforce was both local - mainly day labourers from the countryside - and men from other parts of France, with these workers housed in nearby lodgings. The spread of the railways contributed to the increase of spoken French rather than Breton in some areas. The work was done mostly by hand, with ox and horse-drawn carts to shift the debris. Local farmers sometimes sent buttermilk to sustain the toiling labourers.

The state set general rules for railway construction, but apart from the actual tracks, the individual leasing companies had their own styles of building. On the Réseau Breton the fairly standard station-houses can still be widely seen in their two storey format, made of rendered granite with red brick quoins. Those at halts were smaller, but of similar design. Downstairs was the public area for buying tickets and waiting for trains, whilst the station-master (*Chef de Gare*) and family lived upstairs. Many of these have today been converted into private residences. Other essential buildings at the larger stopping-places included storage for goods, engine sheds and workshops.

Main Lines

In the north

The main lines were built to standard gauge, connecting major centres with widespread business and commercial demands. The northern route from Rennes replaced an original idea for a more central line, with local big-wigs from Morlaix and St-Brieuc lobbying hard to bring the new system through their own towns. As both places lie in deep narrow valleys this meant the challenge of lofty viaducts and stations high above the town centres. The decision came in 1859, and the line to Brest was finished in 1865. It was originally single-track, although pressure of usage finally led to doubling in 1900.

The Compagnie des Chemins de Fer de l'Ouest, originally formed by a consortium of English investors, and later amalgamated with other companies already operating in Normandy, was charged with building and running this network.

Stations from east to west were La Brohinière, Lamballe, St-Brieuc, Guingamp, Plouaret, Morlaix, Landerneau and Brest. In 1872 an extension branched south from St-Brieuc to Pontivy. The stations of Guingamp and Morlaix both served as important connective points with the Réseau Breton.

This was to give a total journey time of 18 hours between Paris and Brest: not exactly TGV speeds, but a distinct boost to commerce and communication at a time when the same trip by road could take up to three days.

Other lines operating within this system went north via Dinan to Dinard from Rennes, and south to Redon.

In the south

Another company, Chemins de Fer de Paris-Orléans, built the southern route from Nantes, with a line through to Quimper in 1863. The main stations were Redon, Questembert, Vannes, Auray and Rosporden. The latter was the main link with the Réseau Breton. The Vannes to Quimper section remained single track until 1901.

Later secondary routes were links to Ploërmel in the east, an important cross-country route via Auray to Pontivy to the north (1864) and one to Quiberon to the south. As early as 1864 the line was extended north from Quimper to Châteaulin, which was taken on to Landerneau a few years later. Pont l'Abbé in Pays Bigouden south of Quimper was also linked to the network.

Réseau Breton
Introduction

After studies in the 1870s, it was decided that further expansion of French railways would proceed on the basis of public utility, with *intérêt general*, bringing significant benefit to a large area, or *intérêt local* for a narrower focus, perhaps bringing a particular tourist hot-spot into connection with the wider network. The latter would rely partly on local investment. Initially the state was to provide subsidies for building these secondary railways in rural France, but in 1883 it was decided to open the development to tender. The state still had to approve the routes, however, and some thought was taken for the future in that the routing of the narrow gauge lines - chosen partly as more economical to construct - should ensure the possibility of later conversion to standard width if required.

The Compagnie des Chemins de fer de l'Ouest bought the concession for a series of lines in Brittany emanating from Carhaix. This Réseau Breton was to be built in narrow gauge, which was more suited to the demanding terrain of cross-country routes serving the less populated areas. It employed more than 500 workers in the 1920s, and covered a total of 427kms, much of which now forms the Green Ways.

This network was intended to serve more rural areas of the centre of Brittany, particularly in places where there were commercial benefits in terms of movement of goods or holiday destinations. It was especially important to link the resources of '*La Ceinture dorée*' or Gold Belt coastal regions with the interior. Vegetables and seaweed based fertilisers were key products on the move.

As landscape determined the actual routes, they often enjoyed attractive scenery, but were not necessarily practically well-placed. A major drawback was that some stations were not near the communities they were supposed to serve. Huelgoat's link was at Locmaria-Berrien and the station for Scrignac and Berrien lies half way between the two.

Carhaix

Carhaix was the hub of this rail network as it had been at the heart of the Roman road system in its earlier incarnation of the important town of *Vorgium*. In Gallo-Roman times and the 19th century it was a focus for agricultural markets. The railway station with its workshop, goods yard, engine sheds and haulage facilities was highly developed, and saw as many as 50 trains a day in the tourist season. All the associated skills like carpentry, paintwork and metal-working were also housed in purpose-built units. More than 500 people were employed in the many aspects of maintenance and repair, and the town blossomed in size and facilities. It's impossible to over-estimate the importance of these rail links, which gave a huge boost to the economy of central Brittany. In 1960 315,000 tons of merchandise moved through Carhaix station.

Network

This consisted of five lines: The first opened in September 1891 from Carhaix to Morlaix, a scenic route of 49kms crossing the hilly skirts of the Monts d'Arrée. This route included the highest point of the network at 213m. The old station on the D42 between Berrien and Scrignac is now a focal point for starting a walk or ride on the Green Way route V7.

To the north-east, a link to Guingamp was opened in September 1893, going via Callac and including the stop of Carnoët-Locarn, which was quite a distance from either of those places, reflecting the planners' problems. This route was extended (and later rebuilt as dual gauge) from Guingamp to the fishing-port of Paimpol. The line is still open today both with ordinary trains, and at certain times, the fine steam train *La Vapeur du Trieux* (vapeurdutrieux.com) running as a tourist excursion between Pontrieux and Paimpol.

The southern arm reached Rosporden in 1896, via a link with the Nantes-Brest canal at Port de Carhaix which had good warehousing facilities, then through Motreff, Gourin and Scaër as well as smaller stopping points. The total length of this branch was 50kms, and Rosporden provided a connection with the main railway line in the south of Brittany. This route is also part of Green Way route V7.

From Carhaix, an important central Brittany line went directly east via Rostrenen (1898) to Loudéac (1902), and was subsequently extended to

La Brohinière (1904) where there was a main line connection, a total distance of 129kms with two main stops and nearly fifty additional halts. To give one example of usage, Carhaix to Loudéac had three return journeys a day in 1955, with the 72kms achieved in 1h 40min. As elsewhere, extra trains were likely to be laid on during the potato season – many small trains were locally called *le train patate*. A fifteen year period on this route at that time recorded over a million passengers.

This is now part of Green Way route V6, running north of Lac de Guerlédan after Gouarec, and then to Mur-de-Bretagne on the way to Loudéac which was also on the main line route originally.

Directly west from Carhaix, the first section to Pleyben via Châteauneuf-du-Faou (or Faon as the station sign mistakenly had it) and Lennon opened in 1904, followed soon after by a connection to Châteaulin. It was decided in 1909 to prolong the line, but owing to WW1, it was not until much later that an important development took the railway out onto the Crozon peninsula, with main stops at Crozon-Morgat (and a link to Le Fret) and the major port of Camaret, the end of the line. When this work was completed in 1925, it made the Réseau Breton the biggest metre gauge network in France. Parts of this track can be walked today, but it has still not been fully developed as a leisure facility.

The terminus at Camaret (in 2010) - the tracks were the other side of the hedge.

Stock

The Réseau Breton initially used steam engines, heavy tank locomotives looking surprisingly similar to the 'Iron Horse' so familiar from Westerns.

These were essentially for passenger trains, and as heavy freight became an increasingly important form of traffic for the railways, more power was required. From 1895 solid and articulated Mallet engines proved their worth on the undulating and sinuous routes, especially for goods trains carrying building stone and other weighty cargoes like fertiliser. The train between Douarnenez and Audierne was known as *Le Train Youtar* – a reference to puffing out steam like belches in a saucepan of porridge (*yout* in the Breton of Cornouaille).

From 1904 new engines with even better powers of traction were purchased, but during WWI many locomotives were requisitioned for use elsewhere.

The first railcar was introduced in 1936, but the war intervened in progress here and it was not until the 1950s, when the Mallet engines were being phased out, that their use became common. These were faster than steam trains and much more sophisticated for passenger comfort, with heating in their wooden cars, where a central gangway separated the seats. A stove was deemed adequate for third class, whereas first and second were served by hot water bottles. Harnessing steam from the engine later replaced both methods, just as oil lamps gave way to electricity.

A famous example still in use for tourists and railway afficionados in Brittany thanks to the Association CFCB (www.cfcb-asso.org/) is the red-and-cream railcar Picasso X3890 which was built in 1953. (The type took its name from a rather distinctive shape.) This train, which covered more than 3,000,000kms in its former career, was carefully restored by enthusiasts and christened 'Ville de Loudéac' after its retirement residence in that town.

Other country routes

There were other narrow gauge lines in western Brittany, organised by department. These connections made easier the often complex challenge of travelling north to south within Brittany.

Finistère took the lead with CFDF (Chemins de Fer Départementaux du Finistère) pushing out from Brest towards the northern coast to Ploudalmezeau and Lannilis, and from Landerneau towards the resort of Brignogan Plage, and another connecting Douarnenez and Audierne.

The important fishing and tourist centre of Concarneau got a link from Quimperlé, and the south-west tip of Brittany was brought onto the railway scene by a freight route from Pont l'Abbé to St-Guenolé. The latter station in the 1950s was in the charge of a Bigouden lady wearing the traditional tall lace headdress of the area. The train on this route to the coast, not known for its speed, was nick-named *birinik* (limpet).

Another company, Chemins de Fer Armoricains, built a route from Morlaix to Plestin-les-Grèves, and a remarkably scenic north/south central Finistère track from Plouescat to Rosporden, over the Monts d'Arrée, highest hills in Brittany. Depending on the load, people sometimes had to get out and walk on the steepest stretches.

In Côtes du Nord (former name of Côtes d'Armor), links from the departmental capital St-Brieuc went up the beautiful Côte de Goëlo to Paimpol, via Plouha with its famous cliffs and beaches. Another provided access to the luxurious resort towns of the Côte Émeraude, very popular with Parisian visitors. There was also a cross-country route from St-Brieuc to Loudéac, where a change at Plémy would provide connection to the historic town of Dinan on the Rance estuary.

Morbihan also saw many metre gauge routes from the CM (*Compagnie des chemins de fer d'intérêt local du Morbihan*) covering more than 400kms in total, with about three return journeys a day on each line. The countryside of the interior was served from Pontivy west to Gourin and east via Josselin to Ploërmel. Important southern commercial links brought in Lorient, Hennebont and Port-Louis, and even the southern land arm of the Gulf of Morbihan with a station at Port Navalo.

The Compagnie des Tramways d'Ille-et-Vilaine operated in eastern Brittany, with links from Rennes to Fougères, Plélan and La Guerche-de-Bretagne developed between 1897 and 1904. A 79km route to the busy port of St-Malo opened in 1909. In the north of this region, the Société des Tramways Breton connected St-Malo with the major shellfish centre of Cancale in 1898.

Economic exploitation

The railway gave sharp impetus to industrial and commercial development, with the Réseau breton in particular doing great service to the formerly rather isolated heart of Brittany. In 1903 a request for a halt at La Folie was refused because there was no specific economic enterprise there to make it commercially worthwhile. In the early years of the 20th century, extra trains from Loudéac served the huge Saturday markets in Rennes and ran on other fair days.

Farmers and merchants soon opened depots near stations, and many co-operatives were formed to exploit these economic facilities, such as that at Lennon in Finistère, where seed potatoes were stored and distributed. The station at Guiscriff in Morbihan helped local quarries to sell their china clay further afield. Rostrenen saw the arrival of lime, seeds and straw, matched by the departure of local grain and stock. In fact, animals were frequently transported for markets, and there was regular movement of horses going to compete at race meetings or to the national studs at Lamballe and Hennebont.

Building materials, such as granite from the Île-Grande and slates from the quarries of Maël-Carhaix were moved within Brittany and beyond, with Paris a major destination for fine quality products. Fertiliser was of major importance to increase yield in central Brittany, and the highly effective seaweed based versions, such as calcium-carbonate and magnesium-rich maërl, could now be brought from the coastal areas without difficulty.

Vegetables, particularly from Léon, and seafood from ports could also circulate with much greater efficiency. Camaret sent fish packed in ice to markets by train: at Châteaulin the load could be transferred to trains for Paris and arrive the next morning.

Social History

The railways certainly played a large part in Brittany's social history in the late 19th and early 20th century. They opened up new opportunities for travel and contacts within Brittany or further afield, such as trips to Paris. Tourism took off in a big way as outsiders were able to visit the magnificent Breton coast and countryside. Seaside resorts, like sophisticated Dinard in the east, developed swiftly with the influx of visitors brought by the railways, and many colourful posters advertised the benefits of idyllic summer holidays with the convenience and ease of travel by train.

Easier access to local markets increased earning potential amongst those of modest means, and seaside holidays or central beauty spots came within the financial reach of ordinary families. After paid holidays for workers began in 1936, coastal resorts with their camping sites or cheap accommodation became sought-after destinations. From 1911 the simple charms of fabulous beaches at Saint-

Nic and Pentrez in the Bay of Douarnenez were only a short trip by the 'bain de mer' train from Carhaix.

Claims for special interests were always an issue, and some communities got rather carried away with the potential. In 1910 the *Conseil Général* made a request to the minister of public works that trains on the Carhaix-Loudéac line should stop long enough at Bon Repos for passengers to visit the ancient abbey. Not surprisingly, this was refused, as such a precedent would disrupt the whole network if others followed suit. Apparently only 12-15 people a day - who may have been locals anyway - were making use of the six trains stopping there.

The railway was for many a symbol of movement, progress and an increasingly fluid society. The mass emigration from Brittany of the late 19th century was helped by the easy rail link to Paris where numerous Bretons settled in the capital or its environs. Within Brittany, special events from fairs and horse-races to distinctively Breton religious pardons were served by special trains which vastly increased the numbers attending.

The railway also found its way into the rich seam of Breton oral culture, perhaps not surprisingly as *chansons de metiers* are common in Breton. Descriptive words vary, with terms such as *marc'h du* or black horse (like the Red Indian Iron Horse), or the traditional term *hent houarn*, along with a frenchised '*cheminod*'. A song by Prosper Proux begins:

> *Ann hend houarn! Ann hend houarn!*
> *Bouzared eo ma diou skouarn;*
> *O kleved ann dud o rakad,*
> *Evel glazarded enn eur prad!*

> The railway! The railway!
> My ears are deafened,
> By passengers clacking away
> Like lizards in a meadow.

Another from 1866 praises the economic benefit of the railway, and its connection with other forms of transport. Interestingly, that other new-found wonder, photography, is also mentioned in the same verse. But it was not all good: from 1891 comes a text in which those staunch Breton religious figures from bygone ages, St Tugdual and St Yves, take a stand against the railway!

On another cultural note, the first *bagad*, or Breton musical band – so important in Brittany today - was formed by railway workers at Carhaix station in 1947. This was a reflection of the socially tight-knit 'clan' of railway workers who often lived in the same area as their colleagues - the name of the quarter called '*négre*' in Carhaix came from the habitually blackened faces of drivers and stokers - and were known for helping each other out. They also banded together in the quest for better working conditions and days limited to 8 hour shifts – there were strikes in 1904, 1910, 1920 and 1938.

Decline

It is a sad fact that better connections with the outside world may not benefit local and regional economies. Roads were improving all the time and, except in comparison with the canals, trains were not that fast – up to 20km an hour on small routes. The lack of facilities at small country stations also meant that lorries were essential in the movement of goods, and after WWI these vehicles were increasingly used for entire journeys as the road network extended. The steady post-WWII rise of private ownership of cars also contributed to the railway's decline, which was equally hit by the rural exodus of the 1960s in Brittany.

Closures for economic reasons had begun in the 1930s, but some lines saw a revival with the demands of the German occupation during WWII. For example, many trains were requisitioned to carry building materials out to the coasts for their elaborate Atlantic Wall constructions. The war saw much damage and destruction to the rail network through aerial attack or local sabotage. In January 1943 the allies bombed the viaduct at Morlaix in the hope of breaking the main Paris-Brest line, but although one arch was hit, the Germans had the trains running again within a fortnight. The railway was a natural target for Breton resistance fighters, who aimed to disrupt communications by burning wagons and tampering with the tracks. This led to a series of derailments such as that at Moustéru where eight cars were overturned in April 1944.

In the 1960s, discussions took place regarding the conversion of narrow gauge lines to standard, but it was hardly an economic proposition with the increasing competition of road haulage and significant investment in Brittany's road network. Only the Carhaix-Guingamp line, still in use today, was upgraded in this way. Buses for passengers and lorries for freight maintained roughly the same services for a while on the other lines, but by May 1967 all lines were closed to passengers, and freight services ended just a few months later.

Engines and machinery were either scrapped or bought by other metre gauge lines elsewhere. By and large the abandoned lines of the Réseau Breton were left, rails removed, to revert to their natural state, although in some places advantage was taken of the groundwork to create minor roads. The station buildings have undergone a variety of changes, many today occupied as private houses or put to other public use. There is a certain irony in the fact that some stations, such as Gourin and Crozon, now house tourist offices.

Revival – the Green Ways

In recent decades former railway tracks of the metre gauge system (and canal towpaths) have been given a new lease of life through metamorphosis into leisure resources for walkers, cyclists and horse-riders. These Green Ways have many advantages, such as secure surfacing, fairly level gradients and increasingly full signage which make them an attractive prospect not only for long-distance trekking, but also for family strolls and disabled use.

Spare a nostalgic thought along those verdant paths for the heat, noise and worthy busyness of the Réseau Breton which made it all possible.

Wendy Mewes

LONG DISTANCE GREEN WAY ROUTES
maps and cycling companion

The V2 and V3 share the same route from St-Malo
to Evran (Écluse du Mottay)

St-Malo is a place of arrivals and beginnings. Both the V2 and the V3 nominally start here but the Green Way itself starts in Dinard, the other side of the Rance. Before taking the ferry to Dinard, the walled city of St-Malo (*Intra-Muros*, or *ville close*) is well worth a detour. Explore the narrow streets, enjoy the pavement cafés, or walk around the ramparts. For the history of St-Malo visit the museum in the château, or the Corsaire's House, 5 rue d'Asfeld (www.demeure-de-corsaire.com).

Getting from St-Malo to Dinard: from the Cale de Dinan, the landing stage at the foot of St-Malo's city walls, there are frequent departures for the 10 minute boat trip to Dinard. Bicycles are accommodated for a small extra charge.

Alternatively, take the boat up the Rance to Dinan, making for an easy, level departure on the V2 or V3 from Dinan (see p.39).

LIASONS:

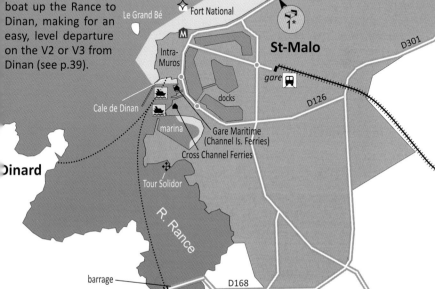

ferry/boat service to Dinard or Dinan.

St-Malo TER Dol-de-Bretagne, Rennes.

Refreshments: Intra Muros - plenty of choice.
Provisions: Intra Muros (no large supermarkets nearby).

The landing stage, Dinard

The Green Way cuts a swathe of relative calm through the busy and commercial hinterland of Dinard and St-Malo. The area is flat, yet not without a morbid interest. During the war the tower of Pleurtuit's church had to go when it interfered with German planes using the aerodrome and in August 1944 Pleurtuit, as a key point in the German defensive perimeter around Dinard and St-Malo, was the scene of a bloody battle with American forces. A lonely monument near La Vieuville marks the site of the heaviest fighting.

Places of interest nearby

- **Barrage de la Rance**. Based on the principles of the tide mills that have been a feature of Brittany since the 12th century, the barrage takes advantage of the exceptionally strong tides, both rising and falling, to generate around 600 million kilowatts per hour of electricity. The barrage also carries the D168 across the Rance.

- **Dinard airport**. As a grass-runway aerodrome between the wars it was the scene of many air displays. In 1940 the Luftwaffe used it as a base for raids on England and it continued to be strategically important though often damaged by allied raids. After the war it was developed as an international airport and is managed by the St-Malo chamber of commerce.

- **Tréméreuc Church** dating from the 12th century.

Signage: ▶S - voie verte Pleurtuit
▶N - V3 Pleurtuit, Dinard.

Route: from the landing stage at Dinard turn left, passing in front of the yacht club and up the slip road. Turn left on Ave George V. Take first right, rue Emile Bara and continue ahead on rue de la Gare. At the top of the hill turn sharp left opposite the new *Bibliothèque* (Place de Newquay, D66). 200m turn right on pathway and follow across open area (old station site), bearing left to beginning of Green Way on former railway track-bed.

Surface: tarmac streets, variable. Former railway compacted sand, good.

Difficulties: most of the Dinard station site is still waste land and obviously due for further development, therefore the above directions are subject to change.

Detours: Dinard the attractive part of town is along the waterfront, especially facing north, an old-fashioned but still fashionable seaside resort. Floral displays and gentle music accompany coast path walkers through Dinard, past Belle-Epoque villas, hotels and restaurants.

Refreshments: Dinard - plenty of choice. Pleurtuit.
Provisions: Dinard, Pleurtuit.

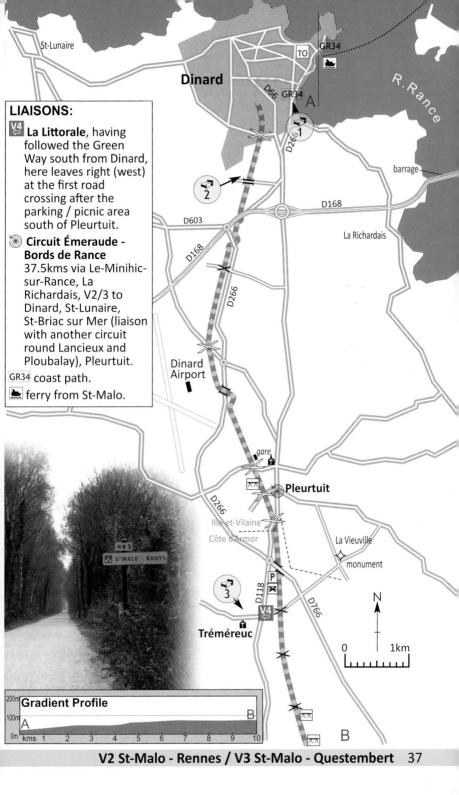

St-Lunaire

Dinard

TO

GR34

D66

GR34 · A

D266

R. Rance

barrage

D168

La Richardais

D603

D168

D266

LIAISONS:

V4 **La Littorale**, having followed the Green Way south from Dinard, here leaves right (west) at the first road crossing after the parking / picnic area south of Pleurtuit.

○ **Circuit Émeraude - Bords de Rance** 37.5kms via Le-Minihic-sur-Rance, La Richardais, V2/3 to Dinard, St-Lunaire, St-Briac sur Mer (liaison with another circuit round Lancieux and Ploubalay), Pleurtuit.

GR34 coast path.

ferry from St-Malo.

2

Dinard Airport

gare

Pleurtuit

D266

Ille-et-Vilaine

Côte d'Armor

La Vieuville

monument

3

D118

P

V4

N

Tréméreuc

0   1km

B

Gradient Profile

200m
100m
0m   kms 1   2   3   4   5   6   7   8   9   10

A

B

V2/V3. 3: Pleslin-Trigavou to Dinan
(15.2kms, Green Way, roads and riverside)
TO Dinan 02 96 87 69 76   www.dinan-tourisme.com

Pleslin-Trigavou is best known for its megalithic alignment, known as the "Druids' cemetery", or "the rock field" (*le champ des roches*). Just a short walk beyond the church, or a longer walk if following the **Circuit des Megalithes** (see liaisons), the alignment consists of 65 monoliths in five rows, set in a grove of oak trees.

Manoir de la Grand' Cour, Taden

At St-Samson-sur-Rance a spectacular leaning menhir awaits megalith hunters. The 'Menhir de la Thiemblaye' stands, or rather leans, at the edge of a wood between the D57 and the railway. It is carved on three sides with various symbols, which in most lights are hard to distinguish. A nearby information panel presents a drawing of them.

The Green Way finishes where the rail track from Dinard meets the still working line from Dinan to Dol. From here the V3 continues on shared roads through the village of Taden, down to the banks of the Rance and along the tow-path to Port de Dinan. The old bridge here is often used as a film set.

Signage: ▶S - V3 Dinan. ▶N - V3 Dinard, Pleurtuit, Trémereuc.

Route: former railway track-bed to St-Samson-sur-Rance, shared roads through Taden to R. Rance, then tow-path to Dinan. (see Difficulties)

Surface: ▶S Green Way compacted sand, good; roads tarmac, variable; tow-path grit or tarmac, fair.

Difficulties: ▶S - Main road crossing at St-Samson, controlled by lights.
V2/3 diversion (poorly signed). Between Dinan and Léhon the towpath (right bank) is closed by a rock fall. At Port de Dinan don't go over bridge but go ahead on road. Under viaduct bear left to carpark and take earth path between carpark and park for camping-cars. This path along bottom of allotments soon rejoins the river bank, all the way to Léhon.
▶N - steep hill between river and Taden.

Detours: Dinan. Medieval walled town with many splendid half-timbered houses. Walk up the street from the bridge and through the Porte de Jerzual.
Menhir de la Thiemblaye, St-Samson-sur-Rance. At traffic lights go east on D57 1.5kms, take path on left, through edge of wood to menhir.

Refreshments: Pleslin-Trigavou, St-Samson-sur-Rance, Taden (camping La Hallerais), Port de Dinan.
Provisions:
Pleslin-Trigavou, St-Samson-sur-Rance, Taden (camping La Hallerais, Easter - mid-Oct.), Dinan.

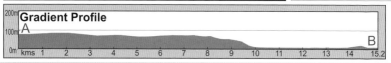

Gradient Profile

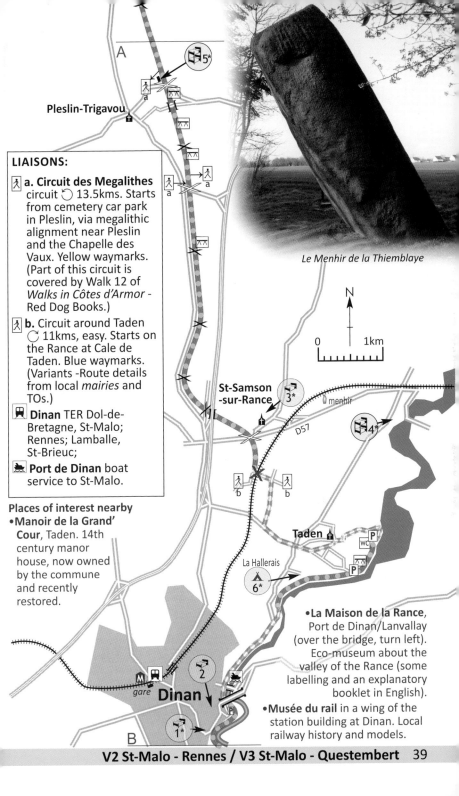

A

Pleslin-Trigavou

⌖

⟐ 5*

☗a ⛺

LIASONS:

🚶 **a. Circuit des Megalithes**
circuit ↻ 13.5kms. Starts
from cemetery car park
in Pleslin, via megalithic
alignment near Pleslin
and the Chapelle des
Vaux. Yellow waymarks.
(Part of this circuit is
covered by Walk 12 of
Walks in Côtes d'Armor -
Red Dog Books.)

🚶 **b. Circuit around Taden**
↻ 11kms, easy. Starts on
the Rance at Cale de
Taden. Blue waymarks.
(Variants -Route details
from local *mairies* and
TOs.)

🚉 **Dinan** TER Dol-de-
Bretagne, St-Malo;
Rennes; Lamballe,
St-Brieuc;

🚢 **Port de Dinan** boat
service to St-Malo.

Places of interest nearby
• **Manoir de la Grand'
  Cour**, Taden. 14th
  century manor
  house, now owned
  by the commune
  and recently
  restored.

☗a 🚶a 🚶

Le Menhir de la Thiemblaye

N

0   1km

**St-Samson
-sur-Rance** ⟐ 3* ⌂ menhir

D57 ⟐ 4*

🚶b 🚶b

Taden ⌖ P WC ⛺ P

La Hallerais ⛺ 6*

• **La Maison de la Rance**,
Port de Dinan/Lanvallay
(over the bridge, turn left).
Eco-museum about the
valley of the Rance (some
labelling and an explanatory
booklet in English).

Ⓜ 🚉 ⟐ 2
gare
Dinan ↓ 🚢 P

⟐ 1*

B

• **Musée du rail** in a wing of the
station building at Dinan. Local
railway history and models.

V2. 4: **Léhon to Evran** (10.7kms, Green Way)
TO Dinan 02 96 87 69 76 www.dinan-tourisme.com

The V2 now follows the Ille-et Rance canal all the way to Rennes. Canal-side cycling is flat, with just an occasional short, stiff climb to get over a road across the canal, but the scenery is constantly changing and there are many interesting diversions to be explored before reaching Brittany's capital city.

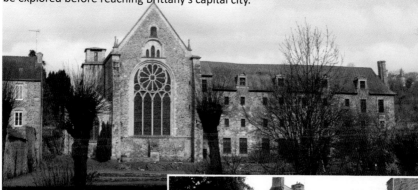

Léhon Abbey from the river

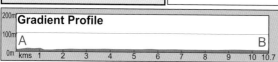

Hairpin bend in Léhon

Signage: ▶S - V3, (V2 from Écluse du Mottay).
▶N - V2 (V3 from Écluse du Mottay) St-Malo, Dinan.

Route: ▶S - path on left bank to Léhon arriving to right of swimming pool and across top of carpark. Signed route through Léhon down to bridge, turning right on road before. Short stretch of road, then continuing on tow-path.

Surface: canal towpath - compacted sand, good. Shared roads - tarmac, fair/good. Pavé in Léhon.

Difficulties: temporary, moveable signs in Léhon V2 switches to opposite side of canal at Evran - easy to miss.

LIAISONS:

St-Malo to Rhuys (see p.50) If coming from Rennes and wishing to link to the V3, the shortest and flattest route is via the Étang de Bétineuc and St-André-des-Eaux. At the far end of the lake there is a choice of three routes (see map), the middle one, though more interesting, may be impractical for cyclists.

a. Sentier du Guinefort direct 26kms, easy. Starts by canal 1km south from Léhon, reaches the V3 between St-André-des-Eaux and Trévron, follows the former railway northwest to beyond Trévron and continues to the flooded valley of the Guinefort. Yellow waymarks. (Route details from local *mairies* and TOs.)

b. Calorguen circuit around the village, easy, cyclable. Variants: 6km yellow waymarks, 15km red waymarks (Route details from local mairies and TOs.)

Gradient Profile

200m
100m
A   B
0m kms 1   2   3   4   5   6   7   8   9   10 10.7

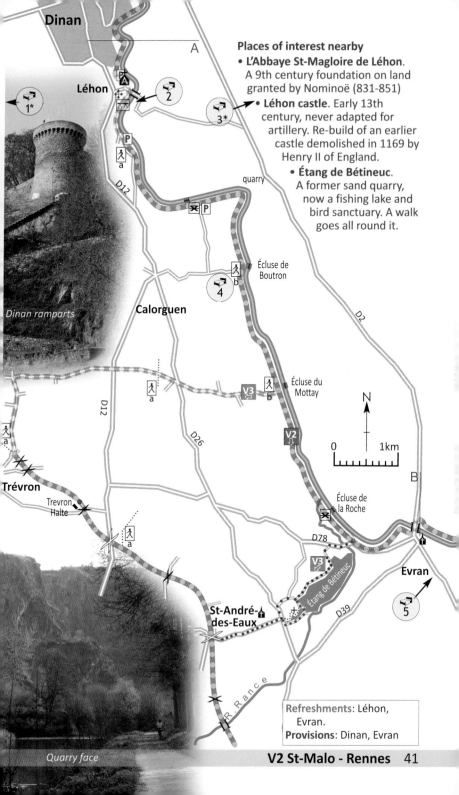

Dinan

A

Léhon

1*

2

3*

Places of interest nearby
- **L'Abbaye St-Magloire de Léhon**. A 9th century foundation on land granted by Nominoë (831-851)
- **Léhon castle**. Early 13th century, never adapted for artillery. Re-build of an earlier castle demolished in 1169 by Henry II of England.
- **Étang de Bétineuc**. A former sand quarry, now a fishing lake and bird sanctuary. A walk goes all round it.

P

a

D12

quarry

P

Dinan ramparts

Écluse de Boutron
b

4

Calorguen

D2

a

V3

Écluse du Mottay
b

V2

N

0   1km

D26

B

Trévron

Écluse de la Roche

Trevron Halte

a

D78

V3

Évran

5

Étang de Bétineuc

a

D39

St-André-des-Eaux

Quarry face

R. Rance

Refreshments: Léhon, Evran.
Provisions: Dinan, Evran

V2. 5: **Evran to Tinténiac** (21.1kms, Green Way)
TO Tinténiac 02 99 68 09 62 (mid June - mid Sept), or websites -
www.combourg.org   www.bretagne35.com   www.paysdelabaie-mtstmichel.com

Again, a change of *département* brings about a change in the way the Green Way is treated. Here in Ille-et-Vilaine the locks on the Ille-et-Rance canal have smart new boards showing their number and name as well as the distance to the next lock in either direction - for the benefit of Green Way users rather than canal traffic. At each major road crossing there is an information panel about the local area, in English as well as French.

For much of the way there is a tow-path, or at least a path, either side of the canal but for comfort it's best to keep to the side signed as the V2. Out of season some parts of the V2 tow-path can be closed for maintenance and it is unfortunately common for no advance warning to be given, entailing a frustrating about-turn back to the last crossing point.

Signage: ▶S - Voie Verte/Canal Ille-et-Rance/Rennes; V2 St-Domineuc, Tinténiac, Hédé.
▶N - V2 St-Domineuc, Evran.

Route: canal tow-path, follow signs for correct side of canal.

Surface: compacted sand, occasional tarmac, good.

Difficulties: V2 switches to opposite side of canal at Evran - easy to miss.

Detours: see liaisons.

LIAISONS:

⚙ A **Circuit des Châteaux** 31kms medium. Starts at St-Domineuc via Trimer, St-Thual, Trévérien (crossing canal), Plesder, Pleugueneuc, then back across canal at St-Domineuc. (Vélo Promenade en Bretagne Romantique No.6, from TOs.)

⚙ B **Circuit du Canal** 24.5kms easy. Starts at St-Domineuc, via D11 to Trémagouët - canal to Tinténiac - Québriac - La-Chapelle-aux-Filzméens - canal back to St-Domineuc (Vélo Promenade en Bretagne Romantique No.5 - from TOs.)

⚙ C **Circuit Duguesclin** 30kms medium. Starts at Tinténiac, across canal then via Bazouges-sous-Hédé, Hédé, St-Symphorien, Les Iffs, Bausserie, Trimer, Tinténiac. (Vélo Promenade en Bretagne Romantique No.4, from TOs.)

🚶⚙ **b. Evran** Circuit ↻ 15kms, links to V3 at Le Quiou (see page 50).

🚶 a **Tour de St Judoce** Circuit ↻ 13kms, yellow waymarks.

Gradient Profile

200m								
100m	A							B
0m	kms 1	2	3	4	5	6	7	7.5

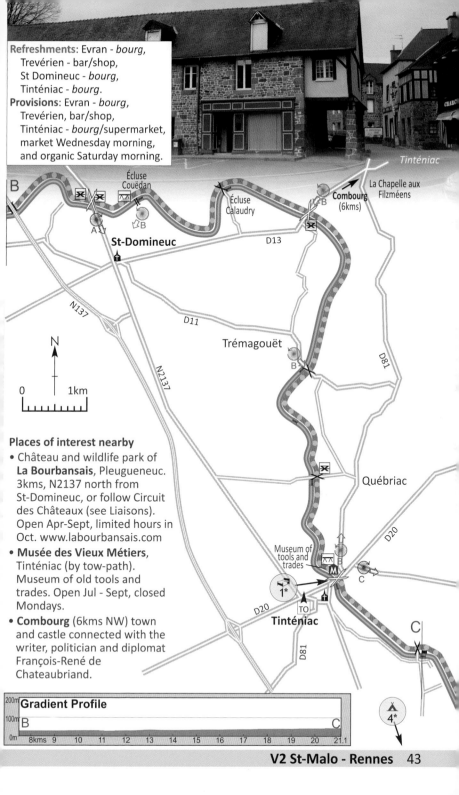

Refreshments: Evran - *bourg*,
   Trevérien - bar/shop,
   St Domineuc - *bourg*,
   Tinténiac - *bourg*.
Provisions: Evran - *bourg*,
   Trevérien, bar/shop,
   Tinténiac - *bourg*/supermarket,
   market Wednesday morning,
   and organic Saturday morning.

Tinténiac

B

Écluse
Couëdan

A
B

St-Domineuc

Écluse
Calaudry

Combourg
(6kms)

La Chapelle aux
Filmméens

B

D13

N137

D11

Trémagouët

N2137

B

D81

N

0   1km

Places of interest nearby
- Château and wildlife park of
  La Bourbansais, Pleugueneuc.
  3kms, N2137 north from
  St-Domineuc, or follow Circuit
  des Châteaux (see Liaisons).
  Open Apr-Sept, limited hours in
  Oct. www.labourbansais.com

- **Musée des Vieux Métiers**,
  Tinténiac (by tow-path).
  Museum of old tools and
  trades. Open Jul - Sept, closed
  Mondays.

- **Combourg** (6kms NW) town
  and castle connected with the
  writer, politician and diplomat
  François-René de
  Chateaubriand.

Québriac

D20

Museum of
tools and
trades

M

C

i*

D20

TO

Tinténiac

D81

C

Gradient Profile

200m
100m
B   C
0m   8kms 9   10   11   12   13   14   15   16   17   18   19   20 21.1

4*

V2. 6: Hédé to St-Médard-sur-Ille (22.3kms, Green Way)
Tourist information - Maison du Canal, La Magdeleine, Hédé (see map)
or www.bretagne35.com or www.paysdelabaie-mtstmichel.com

After Hédé the V2 leaves the tow-path but still follows the canal along a lonely stretch of woodland track from which, initially, one can look down on the last few in the ladder of 11 locks. Then the Bassin de Bazouges can be glimpsed through the trees before the canal turns east and heads across the high ground in a deep cut. As usual in these loneliest of spots where canal construction was at its most laborious, there was a place nearby for the workers that is still called 'le camp'.

Hédé regularly hosts street theatre in mid-August and a weekend jazz festival on the canal in mid-September.

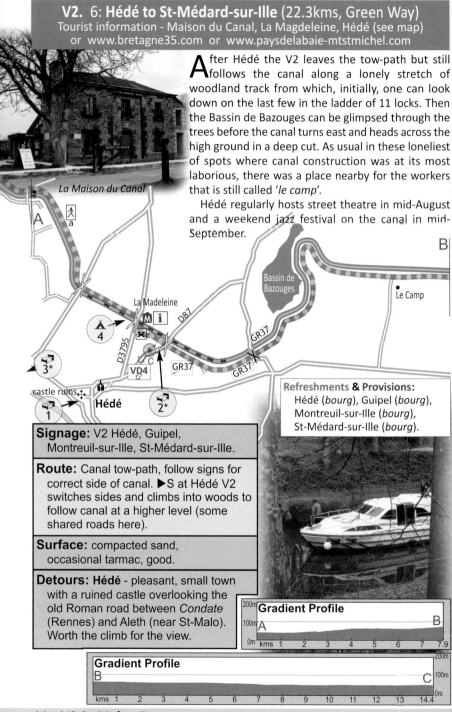

La Maison du Canal

A

La Madeleine

Bassin de Bazouges

Le Camp

D87

GR37

GR37

GR37

B

D3795

VD4

D4

GR37

3*

castle ruins

Hédé

1

2*

Refreshments & Provisions:
Hédé (*bourg*), Guipel (*bourg*),
Montreuil-sur-Ille (*bourg*),
St-Médard-sur-Ille (*bourg*).

Signage: V2 Hédé, Guipel, Montreuil-sur-Ille, St-Médard-sur-Ille.

Route: Canal tow-path, follow signs for correct side of canal. ▶S at Hédé V2 switches sides and climbs into woods to follow canal at a higher level (some shared roads here).

Surface: compacted sand, occasional tarmac, good.

Detours: Hédé - pleasant, small town with a ruined castle overlooking the old Roman road between *Condate* (Rennes) and Aleth (near St-Malo). Worth the climb for the view.

Gradient Profile

200m
100m A — B
0m kms 1 2 3 4 5 6 7 7.9

Gradient Profile

B — C
200m
100m
0m
kms 1 2 3 4 5 6 7 8 9 10 11 12 13 14.4

LIAISONS:

`VD4` **St-Pern - Antrain**, Ille-et-Vilaine cycle route.

🎯 c. **Circuit Duguesclin** (see p.42)

🚶 a. Various circuits, details from local *mairies* and tourist information points.

🚶 **11. Sentier des Guipellois** circuit 8.6kms. Starts in Guipel, Place de l'Église. Waymarked '11' on yellow square (route from www.valdille.fr or local *mairie*).

🚶 **20. Sentier de la Plousière** circuit 7kms via Rigole de Boulet, Étang de Poidevin, Ville Bué and back to canal bridge on the D82. Waymarked 20 on yellow square (route from www.valdille.fr or local mairie).

🚶 **8. Sentier du Bois de Cranne** circuit 14.5kms on west side of canal via Bois de Cranne. Waymarked '8' on yellow square (route from www.valdille.fr or local mairie).

🚶 **7. Sentier de St-Médard** circuit 9.3kms. Starts from the lock at St-Médard, goes to the north of the *bourg* and east of the canal. Waymarked 7 on yellow square (route from www.valdille.fr or local mairie).

Étang de Poidevin

La Plousière

Ville Bué

Guipel

Montreuil-sur-Ille

LIAISONS (cont.):

🚃 **Montreuil-sur-Ille** TER to Rennes; Combourg, Dol-de-Bretagne, St-Malo; Dinan.

🚃 **St-Médard-sur-Ille** TER (as for Montreuil-sur-Ille but less frequent service, stopping trains only).

Places of interest nearby

• **Maison du Canal**, La Madeleine, Hédé. A canal museum in a former lock-keeper's house.

• **Flight of 11 locks** climbing to the highest point on the canal. From the lock beyond the Rigole de Boulet the canal flows in the opposite direction towards the R. Vilaine at Rennes.

• **Château de Montmuran**, Les Iffs (10kms). Historic *château fort* and 17/18th century residence. Open Jun-Sept, pm Sun-Fri. (From Hédé follow cycle route VD4 westwards to Les Iffs.)

St-Médard-sur-Ille

0   1km

N

Bois de Cranne

V2. 7: St-Germain-sur-Ille to Betton (14.8kms, Green Way)
TO Rennes 02 99 67 11 11 www.tourisme-rennes.com
information also available in most local mairies

Since St-Médard the railway has been criss-crossing the canal at a higher level but after St-Germain-sur-Ille it runs alongside the towpath with no fence (beware if you have children or dogs). At the little St-Germain station are the first signs of the approaching big city - commuters' cars in the station car park.

The towns and villages in this area don't feature in most tourist guides - not even St-Sulpice-la-Forêt with its ruined abbey (see Detours and Places of Interest nearby), but the countryside and Rennes Forest offer good walking and a leafy detour.

Lock-gate workshop, St-Germain-sur-Ille

Signage: ▶S - V2 St-Germain, Chevaigné, Betton, St-Gregoire. ▶N - V2 Betton, Chevaigné, St-Germain, Montreuil-sur-Ille.

Route: canal tow-path, follow signs for correct side of canal.

Surface: compacted sand, occasional tarmac, good.

Detours: St-Sulpice-la-Forêt and **Rennes Forest** (Forêt Domaniale de Rennes). Follow the D528 4kms east from Chevaigné, through St-Sulpice-la-Forêt, to the ruined abbey (see Places of interest nearby). Continue to the forest and Étang des Maffrais. Continue on the D528 for almost 1km and at a crossroads in the forest turn sharp right. Continue straight ahead for 6kms, over four major crossroads, to the edge of the forest, and turn right on the D27. Follow it to Betton and the canal.
(See also www.paysderennes.fr - randonnées - Vélo Promenade 5)

LIAISONS:
🚶 **5. Sentier de l'Ille** circuit 13kms. Starts from west end of bridge over canal at St-Germain. Waymarked 5 on yellow square (route from www.valdille.fr or St-Germain mairie).

🚶 **6. Sentier des Roches** circuit 9.5kms. From west end of bridge over canal at St-Germain to the Bois de Cranne. On returning to St-Germain there is also a short (optional) loop up into the *bourg*. Waymarked 6 on yellow square (route from www.valdille.fr or St-Germain mairie).

🚶 **a. Randonnée de la Caleuvre** ↻ circuit 16kms. Starts from Betton along V2 northwards, then east to the Forêt Domaniale de Rennes. Yellow waymarks. Another circuit, blue waymarks, Randonnée du Bois de Betton, 9kms, follows the same outward route. (Details from local mairies and TOs)

🚉 **St-Germaine-sur-Ille** TER Rennes; Montreuil-sur-Ille.

🚉 **Chevaigné** TER Rennes; Montreuil-sur-Ille.

🚉 **Betton** TER Rennes; Montreuil-sur-Ille.

Gradient Profile

200m · 100m · A · · · · · · · · · · · · · B · 0m kms 1 2 3 4 5 6 7 8 9 10 11 12 13 14 14.8

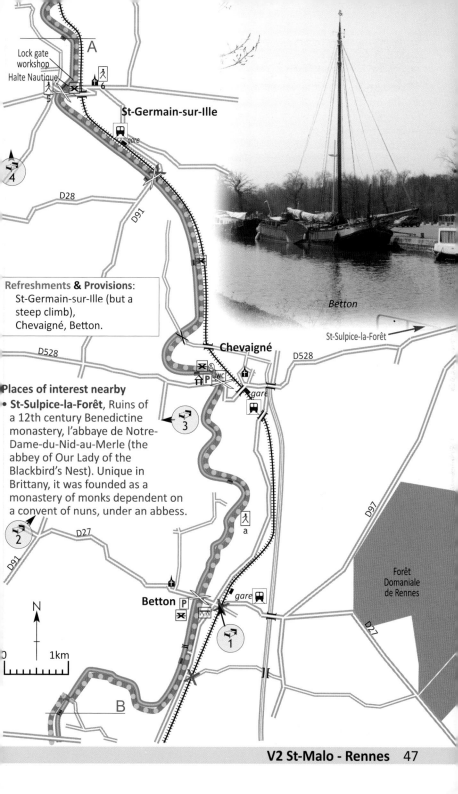

A

Lock gate
workshop
Halte Nautique
5 6

St-Germain-sur-Ille

gare

D28

D91

4

Refreshments & Provisions:
St-Germain-sur-Ille (but a
steep climb),
Chevaigné, Betton.

D528

Chevaigné

P wc

gare

D528

Places of interest nearby
• **St-Sulpice-la-Forêt**, Ruins of
a 12th century Benedictine
monastery, l'abbaye de Notre-
Dame-du-Nid-au-Merle (the
abbey of Our Lady of the
Blackbird's Nest). Unique in
Brittany, it was founded as a
monastery of monks dependent on
a convent of nuns, under an abbess.

3

2

D27

D91

a

D97

Betton

St-Sulpice-la-Forêt

Forêt
Domaniale
de Rennes

N

0   1km

Betton P

gare

1

D27

B

From St-Gregoire the Green Way enters the urban sprawl of Rennes, passing a few areas of industrial waste-land, typical of all large towns. Despite this, the V2 along the tow-path is reasonably pleasant and is used as an open-air resort by local people. It isn't long before it integrates with the street system approaching the city centre. Cycle lanes are in evidence, but are easily missed by anyone unfamiliar with their logic. When in doubt, become a pedestrian and watch the flow of traffic.

Places of interest nearby

• **Rennes**. The old city lies roughly between the Cathedral and the Palais de Justice, Brittany's parliament building. The tourist office is conveniently placed near the south west corner of this area and is signed from the main thoroughfare running east from the end of the Ille-et-Rance canal.

Musée des Beaux Arts - works from the 14th century to the present, including paintings of the Pont-Aven school, Gauguin, Sérusier, etc.

Musée de Bretagne - Brittany and its history.

Signage: ▶S - V2 St-Gregoire, Rennes. ▶N - V2 St-Gregoire, Betton, St-Malo.

Route: canal tow-path into outskirts of Rennes, then streets, mostly with cycle lanes, and still following the canal straight ahead to the R.Vilaine and the city centre.

Surface: ▶S compacted sand, good, then tarmac, variable.

Difficulties: dubious signing at the Écluse St-Martin; there is a walkway under the road but it's narrow and the path soon joins the street on the other side. It's probably better to join the streets at the lock and follow cycle lanes ahead.

Detours: Plenty of choice in Rennes.

Rennes

LIAISONS:

a. Circuit de la Ricoquais ↻ 7kms. Strikes northwards to rejoin the canal opposite le Gacet, then returns along V2 (West bank). Variants from av1 and av2. Green identifier, yellow waymarks. (Route available from local *mairies* and TOs).

b. Circuit de la Boutière ↻ 6.5kms. Around St-Gregoire and returning along V2 from the South. Red identifier, yellow waymarks. (Route available from local mairies and TOs).

Rennes TER trains to...
La Brohinière, Lamballe, St-Brieuc, Guingamp, Plouaret, Morlaix, Landivisiau, Landerneau, Brest.

Redon, Questembert, Vannes, Hennebont, Lorient, Rosporden, Quimper.

Montreuil-sur-Ille, Dol-de-Bretagne, St-Malo.

Dinan; Vitré; Châteaubriant; Nantes.

(And other stations in between)

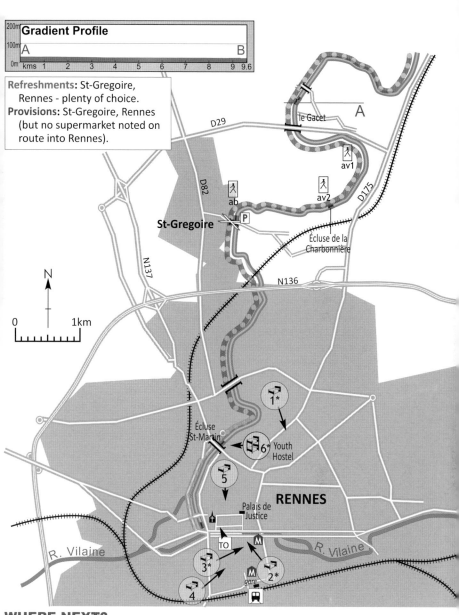

Gradient Profile

200m
100m A _____ B
0m kms 1 2 3 4 5 6 7 8 9 9.6

Refreshments: St-Gregoire,
  Rennes - plenty of choice.
Provisions: St-Gregoire, Rennes
  (but no supermarket noted on
  route into Rennes).

D29   le Gacet   A

av1

D82   av2   D175

ab

St-Gregoire   P

Écluse de la
Charbonnière

N137   N136

N

0   1km

Écluse
St-Martin   1*

6* Youth
Hostel

5

RENNES

Palais de
Justice

TO   M

R. Vilaine   3*   R. Vilaine

M
gare   2*

4

WHERE NEXT?

The V2 is intended to reach Arzal at the mouth of the R. Vilaine but so far it is only
the Ille-et-Rance canal section that is designated as Green Way. Nevertheless, the tow-
path along the Vilaine is cyclable, certainly as far as Redon. (From the end of the
Ille-et-Rance Canal in Rennes, continue ahead to the Vilaine, cross to the far side and
follow the tow-path right.)

The TER from Rennes provides a rail link to many other parts of Brittany, including
points on Green Ways.

The V3 leaves the V2 at the Écluse du Mottay and follows roads to Trévron, where it picks up a former railway going south. A shorter route, which walkers or ornithologists may prefer, would be to continue on the canal for 2kms more, past the Écluse de la Roche, then turning right, away from the canal, where the towpath/lock access road meets the main road (D78). Crossing the river Rance, follow the road right, then bear left into the leisure complex. Here follow round to the big lake (Étang de Bétineuc) and along its northwest side. At the far end of the lake there is a choice of three routes (see map); the more interesting middle one by the ruined chapel may be difficult for cyclists.

V3 1-3. St-Malo to Léhon
see V2, pages 37 - 41

The V3 near Trévron

Signage: ▶S - V3 Calorguen, Rhuys, Trévron, Plouasne.
▶N - V3 St-Malo, Dinan.

Route: left bank (west) of the Rance to Léhon, then a short stretch of road before continuing on the tow-path as far as Écluse du Mottay. Here the V3 leaves the canal to climb to a former railway at Trévron and follow it south. Alternative route via St-André-des-Eaux.

Surface: canal towpath - compacted sand, good. Shared roads - tarmac, fair/good. Former railway from Trévron - compacted sand, initially poor and overgrown, gradually improving towards Le Quiou.

Difficulties: Green Way near Trévron very overgrown.

Detours: Léhon (*Petite Cité de Caractère*). Abbey and medieval castle.

LIAISONS:

St-Malo to Rennes via the canal towpath (see p.41-9).

a. Sentier de Guinefort direct 26kms, easy. Starts by canal 1km south from Léhon, reaches the V3 between St-André-des-Eaux and Trévron, follows the former railway northwest to beyond Trévron and continues to the flooded valley of the Guinefort. Yellow waymarks. (Route details from local *mairies* and TOs.)

b. Evran circuit ↻ 15kms, Starts from Le Quiou via Le Quiou *gare*, north along V3, across to St-André-des-Eaux and Étang de Bétineuc, along canal to beyond Evran, then by roads and tracks back to Le Quiou. (*Walks in Côtes d'Armor*, no.36 - Red Dog Books)

Gradient Profile

A

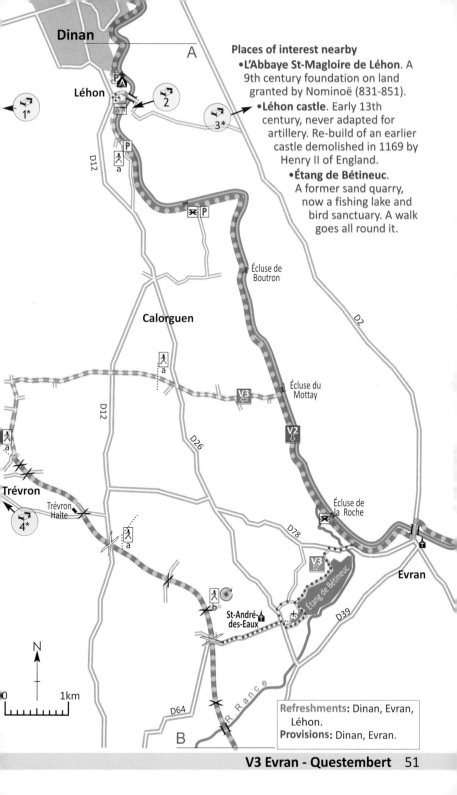

Dinan

A

Léhon

1*

2

3*

D12

P
a

P

Calorguen

D12

D26

D2

Écluse de
Boutron

a

V3

Écluse du
Mottay

V2

Trévron

4*

Trévron
Halte

a

a

b

St-André-
des-Eaux

D78

Écluse de
la Roche

V3

Étang de Bétineuc

Evran

D39

N

0   1km

D64

R. Rance

B

Places of interest nearby
- **L'Abbaye St-Magloire de Léhon.** A 9th century foundation on land granted by Nominoë (831-851).
- **Léhon castle.** Early 13th century, never adapted for artillery. Re-build of an earlier castle demolished in 1169 by Henry II of England.
- **Étang de Bétineuc.** A former sand quarry, now a fishing lake and bird sanctuary. A walk goes all round it.

Refreshments: Dinan, Evran, Léhon.
Provisions: Dinan, Evran.

Several excursions from this section of the Green Way could be rewarding, depending on your interests. The countryside is not too hilly and traffic is not normally too bothersome.

To the west, St-Juvat is renowned for its floral displays in summer, while Tréfumel's church dates from the 11th century and both villages have characterful old houses built of the local honey coloured stone (*pierre de jauge*), a sedimentary limestone originating from shell deposits of the Sea of Falun, which covered this area 15 million years ago. At Le Quiou there is a disused lime kiln, built in 1892 to exploit the same geological phenomenon.

The Château de Hac, at Le Quiou, was built between 1440 and 1448 by Jean Hingant, but in 1450 it was confiscated because of his involvement in the murder of Gilles de Bretagne. The château passed to the Tournemine family and is today still privately owned. Little altered since it was built, it is a fine example of 15th century noble architecture.

To the east, Bécherel is the Breton equivalent of Hay-on-Wye with a dozen or so bookshops in the hilltop village. There is also the site of a castle, dismantled by Henry II of England, and a Celtic, carved stele nestling in a hedge on the eastern outskirts of the village. At the approach to Bécherel, is the Château de Caradeuc with its baroque gardens.

Three and a half kilometres beyond Plouasne the Green Way comes to an end at the D220, after which the railway track is still down and used for the Vélorail (see p.54 & 55).

Le Quiou gare

Signage: ▶S Plouasne, La Boulaie. ▶N Plouasne, Trévron, Dinard.

Route: former railway track-bed all the way - easy to follow.

Surface: compacted sand, good/fair.

Detours: St-Juvat, Tréfumel
A circuit can be made based on the D64 from St-André-des-Eaux (see map p.51) and the D39 to Le Quiou.
Bécherel. Leave the Green Way at Plouasne. Across the border in Ille-et-Vilaine the VD4 passes very close to Bécherel.
GR37. On foot, the GR37 westwards makes a more interesting route to Médréac, 11kms, passing the Grotte à Gabillard and the Alignments of Lampouy (see p.55 & 57).

Places of interest nearby
- **St-Juvat**. Floral displays, old church and stone houses.
- **Tréfumel**. 11th century church, stone houses.
- **Le Quiou**. Excavations of Gallo-Roman villa site, accessible from Green Way. Former lime-kilns on right side of road from station.
- **Château de Hac**. 15th century noble architecture; collection of period furniture, notably chests, four-poster beds and tapestries. (Open Aug & Sept, Sun - Thur pm. Entrance fee, guided visit)
- **Bécherel** (6kms). Bookshops, site of castle, celtic stele.
- **Château de Caradeuc**. Baroque gardens, open July & August, afternoons.

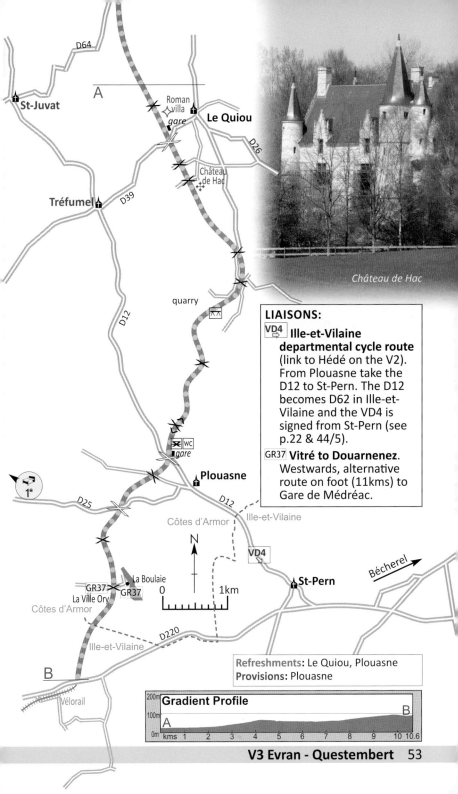

D64

St-Juvat

A

Roman villa
gare
Le Quiou

D26

Château de Hac

Tréfumel

D39

D12

quarry

Château de Hac

LIAISONS:

VD4 **Ille-et-Vilaine departmental cycle route** (link to Hédé on the V2). From Plouasne take the D12 to St-Pern. The D12 becomes D62 in Ille-et-Vilaine and the VD4 is signed from St-Pern (see p.22 & 44/5).

GR37 **Vitré to Douarnenez.** Westwards, alternative route on foot (11kms) to Gare de Médréac.

🍴 WC
■*gare*

Plouasne

D12

Ille-et-Vilaine

Côtes d'Armor

1*

D25

N

VD4

St-Pern

Bécherel

La Boulaie
GR37 GR37
La Ville Ory
Côtes d'Armor

0   1km

D220

Ille-et-Vilaine

B

Vélorail

Refreshments: Le Quiou, Plouasne
Provisions: Plouasne

Gradient Profile

200m

100m
A   B

0m kms 1   2   3   4   5   6   7   8   9   10 10.6

V3. 6: **Médréac to St-Léry** (38.3kms, shared roads, signed route)
TO St-Méen-Le-Grand 02 99 09 58 04 or 02 56 18 02 07
www.pays-stmeen-tourisme.fr

Here the V3 stops being a Green Way and becomes just a cycle route, generally well signed, all the way to St-Léry, just outside Mauron. Stopping points on the way include Médréac, where the old station is a tourist information point as well as the base of Vélorail (see 'Places of interest nearby', p.59). In the beautifully restored waiting room three Breton ladies seem to have been waiting for a train since before the war.

La Brohinière is well-known as a railway junction and here the station still operates for trains on the main line between Rennes and Lamballe, although there is likely to be a more frequent service from the larger town of Montauban-de-Bretagne. The line used by Vélorail now goes no further south than the N12, while the branch from La Brohinière southwards, which later provides a splendid Green Way for the V3, has been restored for freight only as far as St-Léry but is apparently unused. Further on, Mauron station looks very forlorn and neglected. These two developments, Vélorail and the restored line, are of course the reason for this break in the V3's Green Way.

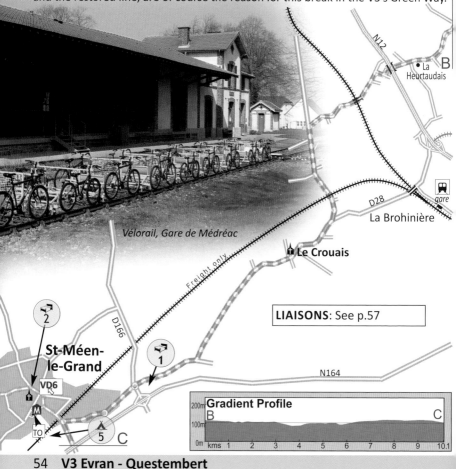

Vélorail, Gare de Médréac

Le Crouais

La Brohinière

gare

La Heurtaudais

B

St-Méen-le-Grand

VD6

LIAISONS: See p.57

Gradient Profile

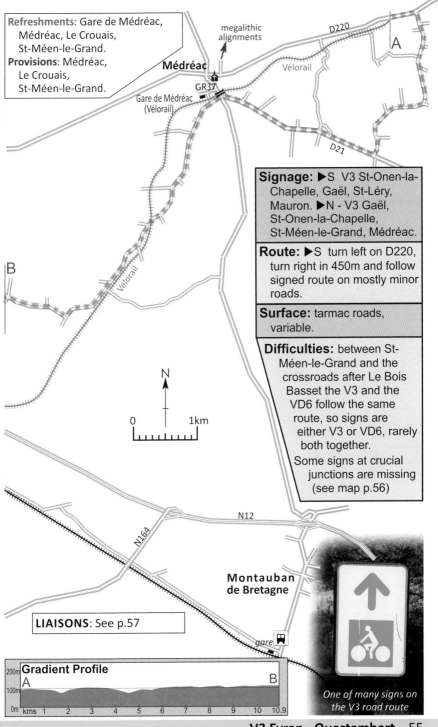

Refreshments: Gare de Médréac, Médréac, Le Crouais, St-Méen-le-Grand.
Provisions: Médréac, Le Crouais, St-Méen-le-Grand.

megalithic alignments

D220

A

Médréac

Vélorail

GR37

Gare de Médréac (Vélorail)

D21

Vélorail

B

Signage: ▶S V3 St-Onen-la-Chapelle, Gaël, St-Léry, Mauron. ▶N - V3 Gaël, St-Onen-la-Chapelle, St-Méen-le-Grand, Médréac.

Route: ▶S turn left on D220, turn right in 450m and follow signed route on mostly minor roads.

Surface: tarmac roads, variable.

Difficulties: between St-Méen-le-Grand and the crossroads after Le Bois Basset the V3 and the VD6 follow the same route, so signs are either V3 or VD6, rarely both together.
Some signs at crucial junctions are missing (see map p.56)

N

0   1km

N12

N164

Montauban de Bretagne

LIAISONS: See p.57

gare

Gradient Profile
200m
100m
A   B
0m kms 1   2   3   4   5   6   7   8   9   10 10.9

One of many signs on the V3 road route

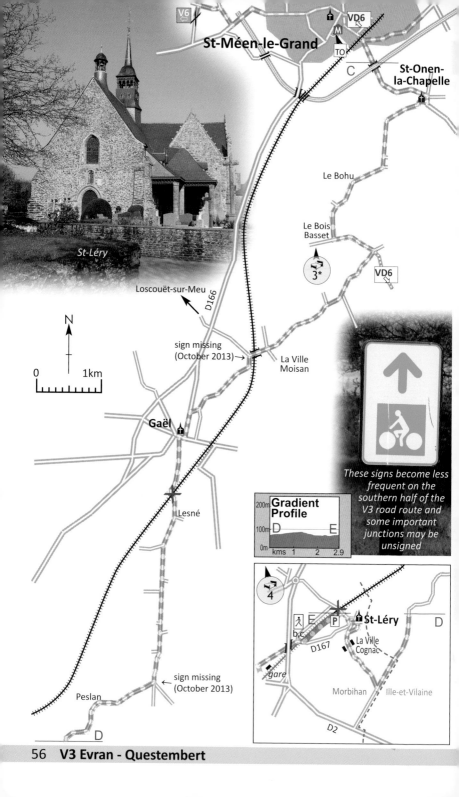

V6

VD6

St-Méen-le-Grand

TO

C

St-Onen-la-Chapelle

Le Bohu

Le Bois Basset

3*

VD6

St-Léry

Loscouët-sur-Meu

D166

N

0   1km

sign missing (October 2013) →

La Ville Moisan

Gaël

Lesné

These signs become less frequent on the southern half of the V3 road route and some important junctions may be unsigned

Gradient Profile

200m
100m D ———————————— E
0m   kms 1   2   2.9

4

E

b,c

P

St-Léry

D

D167

La Ville Cognac

gare

Morbihan   Ille-et-Vilaine

← sign missing (October 2013)

Peslan

D2

D

Places of interest nearby

- **Médréac** *gare* and **Vélorail**. A sort of go-cart on rails, propelled by two mountain bikes, can be hired for a trip along the old railway. Also a railcar for non-pedallers and a tourist train (by road) that visits Médréac and the Alignments of Lampouy.
- **Megalithic alignment of Lampouy**. (See Detours) Almost 50 menhirs are spread in groups over several fields, oriented NNW to SSE.
- **La grotte à Gabillard** (Gabillard's cave) The GR37 passes close to la Grotte à Gabillard before going on to the alignments of Lampouy. Jean Julien Gabillard was a Chouan (see p.8) who took refuge here.
- **St-Méen-Le-Grand** (see p.90-1). **Abbatiale** (abbey church), guided visits from the Tourist Office. **Musée Louis Bobet** (same address as TO) retracing the career of the great French champion cyclist, a native of St-Méen.
- **St-Léry**. The 14th/16th century church contains a few elements saved from the old chapel of Barenton (in Brocéliande) which had been demolished by church authorities as it had been tainted by the mid-12th century heresy of Eon de l'Étoile, a mad monk who thought he was the Messiah but behaved like a brigand, taking possession of church property and redistributing it to his followers.
  In the walls of some of the houses in La Ville Cognac (St-Léry, on route) there are large carved stones that come from the ruins of Mauron castle (demolished by order of DuGuesclin in 1373).
- **Gaël**. The church has an 11th century nave.

LIAISONS:

V6 St.Méen-le-Grand to Carhaix.

VD6 the Ille-et-Vilaine cycle route that links the V6 from Carhaix to its designated end at Vitré.

GR37 Vitré - Douarnenez. Passes through Médréac.

La Brohinière or **Montauban de Bretagne**, TER, Rennes, Lamballe, St-Brieuc.

Detours: Alignments of Lampouy. (4kms) From Médréac station follow the road into Médréac, turn right in the centre, pass the church and turn left on Route de Néal. Follow signs to the alignments, or if walking follow the GR37 via Grotte à Gabillard (see Places of interest nearby).

Loscouët-sur-Meu. At the bridge over the railway NE of Gaël, leave the cycle route by the road NW, cross over the D166 and carry straight on to Loscouët. Here it is possible to join a cycle promenade (waymark: thin white arrow on dark green rectangle) based on the V6 (St-Méen-le-Grand to Carhaix). This makes a direct link from the V3 to the V6 avoiding St-Méen-le-Grand.

Green Way again, St-Léry

Refreshments: St-Méen-Le-Grand, St-Onen-La-Chapelle, Gaël, Mauron.
Provisions: St-Méen-Le-Grand, St-Onen-La-Chapelle, Mauron.

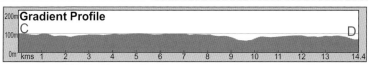

Gradient Profile

200m
C
100m
D
0m   kms 1   2   3   4   5   6   7   8   9   10   11   12   13   14.4

Back on the Green Way and this time with tarmac. Morbihan made an early decision to invest in tarmac and that must have paid off in reduced maintenance costs. For walkers who find tarmac a little hard on the knees there is a 1 metre cinder track alongside, and this does tend to get grassed over where it's less frequently used.

Don't look for the Mauron tourist office in the town centre; it's in a lay-by on the D766 which by-passes the town. It is accessible from the Green Way, across the public park known as La Folie. There is a self-service cycle maintenance kiosk at the entrance to the park from the Green Way.

Mauron lies just north-west of the Forêt de Paimpont, otherwise known as Brocéliande, steeped in Arthurian legend but also worth exploring for its own sake, hiding a few dolmens and remarkably old oak trees.

Signage: ▶S - V3 Loyat, Ploërmel, Malestroit, Questembert. ▶N - V3 Mauron.

Route: new Green Way from St-Léry, beside railway, then roads to Mauron *gare*. From Mauron, former railway track-bed, easy to follow.

Surface: tarmac, good on Green Way, but only fair on roads around Mauron *gare*.

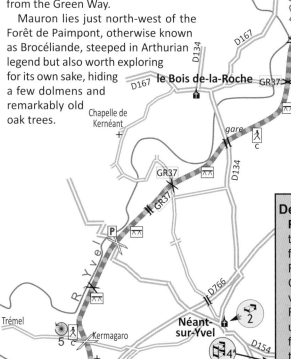

Difficulties: in Mauron, sign missing from end of Rue de la Gare to beginning of Green Way - bear left to find Green Way.

Detours: le Bois de la Roche. Near St-Guinel, turn right on the road, following the GR37. Follow the road (or the GR if walking) to the village of Le Bois de la Roche. In the centre, pick up the GR37 again and follow it on the road, via the Chapelle de Kernéant, back to the Green Way.

Tréhorenteuc and the **Forêt de Brocéliande**. (5.5kms to Tréhorenteuc via Néant-sur-Yvel) Leave the Green Way where the GR37 rejoins (signed , Tréhorenteuc). Continue through Néant on the D154 to Tréhorenteuc.

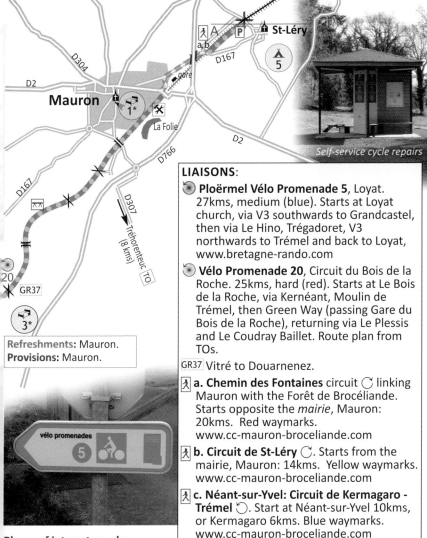

St-Léry

Mauron

La Folie

Self-service cycle repairs

Tréhorenteuc TO (8 kms)

GR37

Refreshments: Mauron.
Provisions: Mauron.

vélo promenades
5

LIAISONS:

Ploërmel Vélo Promenade 5, Loyat. 27kms, medium (blue). Starts at Loyat church, via V3 southwards to Grandcastel, then via Le Hino, Trégadoret, V3 northwards to Trémel and back to Loyat, www.bretagne-rando.com

Vélo Promenade 20, Circuit du Bois de la Roche. 25kms, hard (red). Starts at Le Bois de la Roche, via Kernéant, Moulin de Trémel, then Green Way (passing Gare du Bois de la Roche), returning via Le Plessis and Le Coudray Baillet. Route plan from TOs.

GR37 Vitré to Douarnenez.

a. Chemin des Fontaines circuit ↻ linking Mauron with the Forêt de Brocéliande. Starts opposite the *mairie*, Mauron: 20kms. Red waymarks. www.cc-mauron-broceliande.com

b. Circuit de St-Léry ↻. Starts from the mairie, Mauron: 14kms. Yellow waymarks. www.cc-mauron-broceliande.com

c. Néant-sur-Yvel: Circuit de Kermagaro - Trémel ↻. Start at Néant-sur-Yvel 10kms, or Kermagaro 6kms. Blue waymarks. www.cc-mauron-broceliande.com

Places of interest nearby

- **Tréhorenteuc** and the **Forêt de Brocéliande** (see Detours). A mystic forest steeped in the legends of King Arthur and Merlin. See the Tree of Gold, the Valley of No Return and the House of Viviane. (broceliande.valsansretour.com)

- **Château de Comper** (8kms E, from Mauron via D2 through Concoret) Centre Arthurien, exhibitions, bookshop, events with an Arthurian or celtic theme. (Open in season.) (http://centre-arthurien-broceliande.com)

- **Le Bois de la Roche** (see Detours). An interesting village with a church dating from the 15th century and a château that was pillaged and occupied by Leaguers c.1598 and at the revolution was the scene of a clash between *chouans* and Republicans.

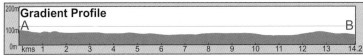

Gradient Profile

200m
100m
0m kms 1 2 3 4 5 6 7 8 9 10 11 12 13 14.2

A   B

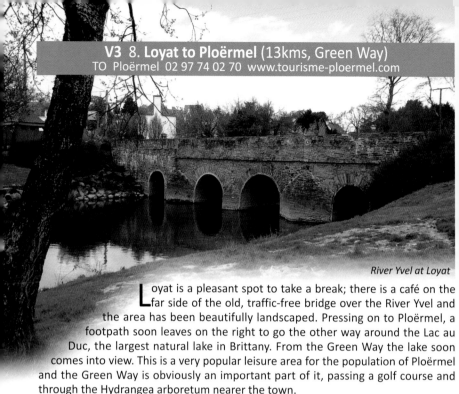

V3 8. Loyat to Ploërmel (13kms, Green Way)
TO Ploërmel 02 97 74 02 70 www.tourisme-ploermel.com

River Yvel at Loyat

Loyat is a pleasant spot to take a break; there is a café on the far side of the old, traffic-free bridge over the River Yvel and the area has been beautifully landscaped. Pressing on to Ploërmel, a footpath soon leaves on the right to go the other way around the Lac au Duc, the largest natural lake in Brittany. From the Green Way the lake soon comes into view. This is a very popular leisure area for the population of Ploërmel and the Green Way is obviously an important part of it, passing a golf course and through the Hydrangea arboretum nearer the town.

There are numerous circuits for both walkers and cyclists (see Liaisons) and it would be quite possible to set out on one and switch to another half way round, either by accident or design, so a visit to the TO in Ploërmel to pick up plans of the various routes is recommended.

Continuing south from the old engine sheds and station at Ploërmel, one is reminded what an important railway junction this was, as the Green Way passes in turn the branches eastwards to Messac (now a Green Way) and west via Josselin. Finally in this section the River Ninian comes from the right, having absorbed the River Yvel, and will remain with the V3 until they reach the Nantes-Brest Canal, the one to flow into it, the other to pass over it.

Ploërmel engine sheds

Places of interest nearby

- **Ploërmel**. Little remains of the ramparts of the town but there is one tower on the edge of a car park. Of the interesting old houses in Ploërmel, one belonged to the Dukes of Brittany and dates from the 12th century, another from the 16th century is the Café des Quatre Soldats, formerly the Hôtel Le Goasbé. An impressive astronomical clock is on display in the courtyard of the Lycée La Mennais and the museum here has a 3D film (English version available) to explain how it works.

- **Chapelle St-Golven**, Le Vieux Bourg. An architecturally interesting chapel dating from the 12th/14th century and with a curious tower. (See Detours and Liaisons  c.)

- **Rocks** and *allée couverte* of La Ville Bouquet, on a wooded scarp overlooking the River Ninian (see Liaisons ⽊ c. Other megaliths can be found on the various circuits).

- **Manoir de Lézonnet** (next to Green Way at northern end of Lac au Duc). The house is 19th century, replacing an earlier manor house, but the site was originally a feudal castle, of which one watchtower and the chapel remain.

- **Monument to the Battle of the Thirty** (see Detours), commemorating a battle that took place in 1351 during Brittany's War of Succession between Charles de Blois, backed by the French, and the Montforts, supported by the English. By agreement, thirty knights from each of the opposing garrisons of Josselin and Ploërmel met for a pitched battle half way between the two towns. All the knights were either killed or wounded but the pointless victory went to the supporters of Charles de Blois from Josselin. The chapel at St-Maudé, 1.5kms to the north, is said to have been built where the fallen knights were buried.

Signage: ▶S - V3 Ploërmel, La Chapelle C(aro) *gare*, Malestroit, Questembert. ▶N - V3 Ploërmel, Loyat, Mauron.

Route: former railway track-bed all the way - easy to follow.

Surface: tarmac, good.

Difficulties: likely to be crowded around Ploërmel on Sundays and holidays

Detours: to Chapelle St-Golven, Le Vieux Bourg en Taupont. From the roundabout at Ploërmel *gare* take the D724 to Josselin. Follow it right to avoid joining the N24, bear right over the old bridge at Pont Neuf and turn right to Le Vieux Bourg and its chapel. Return the same way, or continue on the D724 to Josselin (6kms), passing the monument to the Battle of the Thirty half way.

Josselin is a small medieval city with an impressive castle that can be visited and also has a doll museum.

Sunday afternoon near Loyat

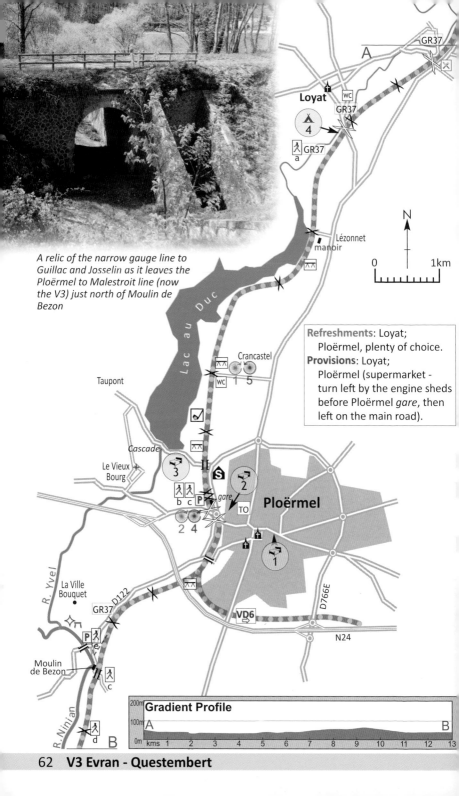

A relic of the narrow gauge line to Guillac and Josselin as it leaves the Ploërmel to Malestroit line (now the V3) just north of Moulin de Bezon

Refreshments: Loyat;
Ploërmel, plenty of choice.
Provisions: Loyat;
Ploërmel (supermarket - turn left by the engine sheds before Ploërmel *gare*, then left on the main road).

Loyat

Lézonnet manoir

Crancastel

Taupont

Cascade

Le Vieux Bourg

Ploërmel

La Ville Bouquet

Moulin de Bezon

N

0   1km

Gradient Profile

V3 8. Loyat to Ploërmel

LIAISONS:

 Vélo Promenade 1, Ploërmel - Gourhel. 20kms, easy. Starts at Ploërmel *gare*.
www.bretagne-rando.com

 Vélo Promenade 2, via Taupont, around the Lac au Duc. 20kms, easy. Starts at roundabout by Ploërmel station.
www.bretagne-rando.com

Start of the VD6 Green Way to Messac (left)

 Vélo Promenade 4, Taupont - Guillac. 27kms, medium. Starts at Taupont church or by Ploërmel station.
www.bretagne-rando.com

 Vélo Promenade 5, Loyat. 27kms, medium. Starts at Loyat church, via V3 southwards to Crancastel (aka. Grandcastel, Grand Castel), then via Le Hino, Trégadoret, Green Way to Trémel and back to Loyat.
www.bretagne-rando.com

 Ploërmel to La Trinité-Porhoët, 27kms, direct, easy. Named "Le Petit Pelot" after the train that used to link Ploërmel to La Trinité-Porhoët.
www.tourisme-ploermel.com

VD6 **Ploërmel to Messac** (Green Way) leaves from the summit (pictured above) south of Ploërmel. After Guer it enters Ille-et-Vilaine as VD2 (See p. 19 & 21)

GR37 **Vitré to Douarnenez**. South of Ploërmel the GR37 joins the D122 beside the V3. This is an easier and more interesting place to join the GR37 than at the inviting sign further south (Guillac 6, Josselin 10), which is only a *link to* the GR37. That link is not signed after leaving the V3 and you would miss the *allé couverte* and *rochers* of La Ville Bouquet.

 a. **Tour du Lac au Duc** circuit ⟳ 14kms. Starts in the parking of the Hôtel Roi Arthur at the southern tip of the Lac au Duc.

 b. **Le Chemin du Diable au Paradis des Hortensias** (The Devil's Way to Hydrangea Heaven) circuit ⟳ four possible combinations up to 7.6kms. Starts at Ploërmel station. The park (through which the Green Way passes) to the east of the Lac au Duc, is famous for its many varieties of Hydrangea.

 c. **Chapelles & Megalithes** circuit ⟳ 13kms. Starts at the Cascade du Lac au Duc, takes a long loop south to cross under the V3 at Moulin de Bezon and returns to Ploërmel by the VD6 Green Way.

Ploërmel gare

 d. **Chapelles & Croix** circuit ⟳ 17kms. Starts near the roundabout, junction of N24 and D766E, follows former railway (VD6 Green Way) westwards, then turns left across N24. Joins V3 near Moulin de Bezon, follows V3 south, then leaves east to rejoin VD6 beyond start and return.

 e. **Les Voies des Deux Rivières** circuit ⟳ 11kms. Starts from parking on north side of D122 bridge over River Ninian. Follows GR37 southwards, then joins Nantes-Brest canal at Écluse de Blond. Returns up V3 with a diversion via Le Roc Brien and Croix Dom Jan.

V3 9. **Montertelot to Malestroit** (11.6kms, Green Way)
TOs Ploërmel 02 97 74 02 70 www.tourisme-ploermel.com
Malestroit 02 97 75 14 57 www.ccvol.com/-Tourisme-.html

Here the V3 flirts with the V1 as the railway crosses over a couple of loops in the Nantes-Brest Canal and it's very tempting to switch one's allegiance for a few kilometres and follow the canal. Either way you will be passing through the valley of the River Oust, where lush meadows stretch away on either side, surrounded by distant wooded hills. The waterfront at Montertelot is particularly attractive, while the long stone bridge at Le Roc St-André is best viewed from the south. If approaching along the V3 from Malestroit, to join the canal take the linking path on the right, immediately after the tunnel under the N166.

Once the V3 has crossed the canal for the last time it begins to climb to the Gare de Malestroit (see next section), 50m above the town. If coming from the north and a visit to the town is scheduled at the end of a long day, it's easier to go via the canal.

Places of interest nearby

• **Malestroit**. A delightful canal-side town with a medieval centre. Visit the church of St-Gilles, dating from the 12th century, with interesting animal carvings around the south door. Over the river on the road to Ploërmel are the remains of La Chapelle de la Madeleine, where the Treaty of Malestroit was signed in 1343, bringing a temporary peace in the 100 Years War.

• **Manoir du Vaugace**, restored 15th century manor, open in season, except 24th July - 12 August.

Signage: ▶S - V3 La Chapelle C. *gare*, Malestroit *gare*, Questembert.
▶N - V3 Ploërmel, Mauron.

Route: former railway track-bed all the way - easy to follow.

Surface: tarmac, good.

Detours: Malestroit (best approached from the canal).
La Touche Carné - pretty village worth a little tour. Look for a restored 15th century manor and a ruined mill.
Manoir du Vaugace (near Malestroit - see 'Places of interest nearby').

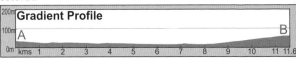

Gradient Profile

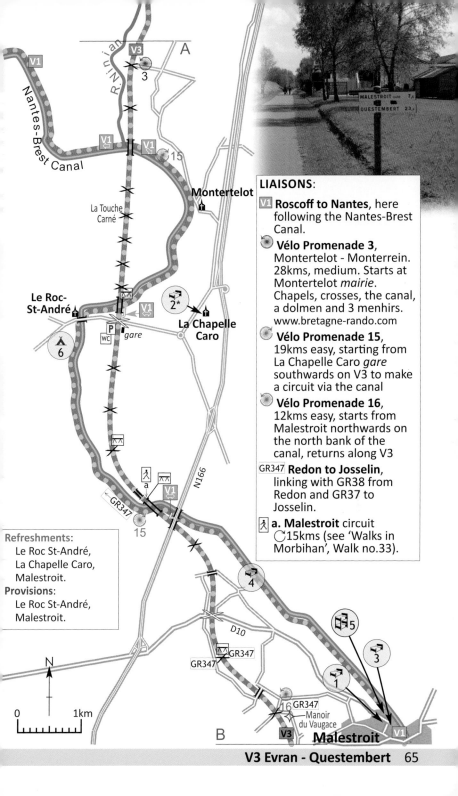

V1 Nantes-Brest Canal

V3 3

V1

V1 15

Montertelot

La Touche Carné

Le Roc-St-André

2*

La Chapelle Caro

P
WC   *gare*

6

a

V1

GR347

15

N166

Refreshments:
Le Roc St-André,
La Chapelle Caro,
Malestroit.
Provisions:
Le Roc St-André,
Malestroit.

4

5

GR347
GR347

3

1

N

0   1km

D10

16   GR347
—Manoir
du Vaugace

V3   **Malestroit**   **V1**

LIAISONS:

V1 **Roscoff to Nantes**, here following the Nantes-Brest Canal.

Vélo Promenade 3, Montertelot - Monterrein. 28kms, medium. Starts at Montertelot *mairie*. Chapels, crosses, the canal, a dolmen and 3 menhirs. www.bretagne-rando.com

Vélo Promenade 15, 19kms easy, starting from La Chapelle Caro *gare* southwards on V3 to make a circuit via the canal

Vélo Promenade 16, 12kms easy, starts from Malestroit northwards on the north bank of the canal, returns along V3

GR347 **Redon to Josselin**, linking with GR38 from Redon and GR37 to Josselin.

a. Malestroit circuit ↻15kms (see 'Walks in Morbihan', Walk no.33).

V3 10. **Malestroit to Molac** (12.1kms, Green Way)
Malestroit 02 97 75 14 57 www.ccvol.com/-Tourisme-.html
Questembert 02 97 26 56 00 www.rochefortenterre-tourisme.com

Although the tarmac has been down for some years now and is still in good condition there have been more recent developments of the Green Way's facilities.

The car park and picnic area at Malestroit on the barely recognisable old station site was completed in the spring of 2010 and there are now more signed *Vélo Promenades*. Details of these, with route maps, are available from local tourist offices.

This stretch of the Green Way linking the communes of Malestroit, Pleucadeuc and Molac passes through idyllic countryside, crossing the few main roads rather than running endlessly alongside them. On passing the deep valley of Le Petit Gournava, one can be thankful for the Green Way's gentle gradients.

The Landes de Lanvaux are marked by a change in the trackside vegetation, mature beech and oak giving way to a more open landscape of gorse, birch and little oak trees.

Signage: ▶S - V3 Pleucadeuc *gare*, Questembert, Rhuys.
▶N - V3 Pleucadeuc *gare*, Malestroit.

Route: former railway track-bed all the way - easy to follow.

Surface: tarmac, good.

Difficulties: finding the car park at Malestroit *gare* - its road entrance is off the roundabout, shared with that of the Super-U supermarket.

Detours: (on foot - possibly cycle if dry) **Chapelle St-Barthélémy** and **La Pierre Branlante.** At the third crossing south of the River Claie, take the Circuit de St-Marc to the west and follow it (yellow waymarks) back to the V3 where the GR38 crosses.
Le Chapeau de Roche. From the summit of the Landes de Lanvaux take the D149 towards Pleucadeuc for 1km and turn left towards La Crolaie. Return to the V3.

LIAISONS:

Vélo Promenade 18, 24kms medium, starts from Malestroit northwards along canal but soon climbs SW to the V3 near St Marcel. Returns along canal from south of St Congard.

Vélo Promenade 22, 22kms energetic, starts in Pleucadeuc and explores countryside northwards.

30(formerly 9). **Circuit de St-Marc** circuit ○ 22kms. Starts from Pleucadeuc, goes north to Chapelle St-Marc, southwest to V3, then a loop to the east of the V3 followed by a loop to the west before returning to Pleucadeuc. Yellow waymarks, route plan from Questembert TO.

7/8. Circuit du Lindeul circuit ○ 11kms. Starts from Molac, goes south to meet the V3 and follow it south for 1km, then loops east of the V3, returning to follow it north for 1km before returning to Molac. Yellow waymarks, route plan from Questembert TO.

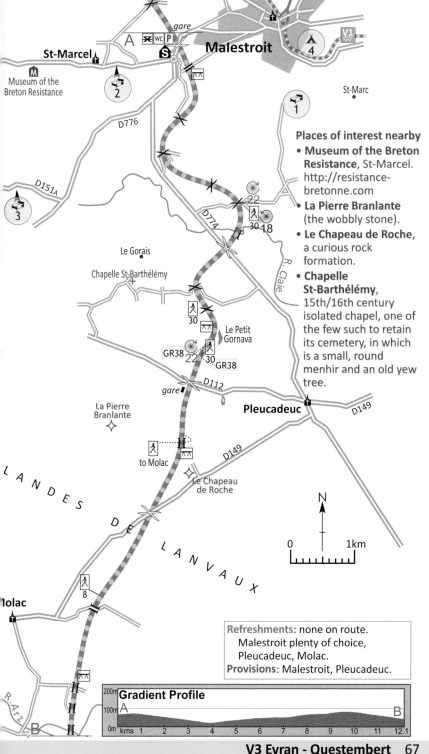

St-Marcel

Museum of the
Breton Resistance

Malestroit

St-Marc

Places of interest nearby
- **Museum of the Breton Resistance**, St-Marcel. http://resistance-bretonne.com
- **La Pierre Branlante** (the wobbly stone).
- **Le Chapeau de Roche**, a curious rock formation.
- **Chapelle St-Barthélémy**, 15th/16th century isolated chapel, one of the few such to retain its cemetery, in which is a small, round menhir and an old yew tree.

Le Gorais

Chapelle St-Barthélémy

Le Petit Gornava

GR38   22   30   GR38

gare   D112

Pleucadeuc   D149

La Pierre Branlante

to Molac

Le Chapeau de Roche

D149

N

0   1km

L A N D E S   D E   L A N V A U X

Molac

R. Arz

Refreshments: none on route.
Malestroit plenty of choice,
Pleucadeuc, Molac.
Provisions: Malestroit, Pleucadeuc.

Gradient Profile
200m
100m
0m   kms 1   2   3   4   5   6   7   8   9   10   11   12.1
A   B

Now over the Landes de Lanvaux but still another hill to climb before the end of the Green Way. Surprisingly, Questembert is even higher, at over 100m. The road from the Green Way to the Bel Air roundabout is quiet, except perhaps on race days, and the main road into Questembert has a cycle lane at the side for most of the way, although very narrow in the underpass beneath the railway. At the traffic lights, turn right to find the back way into the town centre, passing a convenient supermarket. Market day is Monday, when the 16th century, timber-framed covered market fulfils its purpose. The tourist office is opposite the far end, on the left.

Market day in Questembert

Signage: ▶S - V3 Questembert. ▶N - V3 Molac, Pleucadeuc, Malestroit.

Route: former railway track-bed all the way to Bel Air, then road with cycle lane.

Surface: tarmac, good. (The Green Way is better than the road into Questembert)

Difficulties: some double barriers set too close.

Detours: Moulin de Lançay, either there and back or following Vélo Promenade 21.
Chapelle du Lindeul, just a short break from the Green Way.

Places of interest nearby

- **Questembert**, for its 17th century covered market, still in use. Also the nearby Tourist Office in the 15th/16th century Hôtel Belmont. See the rear of the building for its tower with the elaborate roof which includes two carved wooden caryatides representing Questembert and his wife.

- **Moulin de Lançay**, a centuries-old restored working mill. Guided visits (3€). Open Sunday & bank holiday afternoons May, June & Sept; Thursday to Sunday afternoons in July & August. (see Liaisons: Vélo Promenade 21.)

- **Chapelle du Lindeul**. The Knights of Malta originally built this chapel in the 13th century. It was re-built in the 19th century. (See Liaisons: Circuit du Lindeul.)

LIAISONS:

Vélo Promenade 21, Molac. 21kms, energetic. Starts from V3. at Le Guernet. Chapels, mills (inc. de Lançay) and the *bourg* of Molac. Route plan from Questembert TO.

Vélo Promenade 23, Questembert. 21kms, medium. Starts from entrance to hippodrome, beginning of v.v. at Bel Air. Passing several chapels and the Menhir de la Pierre Longue. Route plan from Questembert TO.

7/8. Circuit du Lindeul 11kms. Starts from Molac (see p.66/7), goes south to meet the V3 and follow it south for 1km, then loops east of V3, returning to follow it north for 1km before returning to Molac. Yellow waymarks, route plan from Questembert TO.

Questembert. TER, Vannes, Quimper; Redon; Rennes; Nantes.

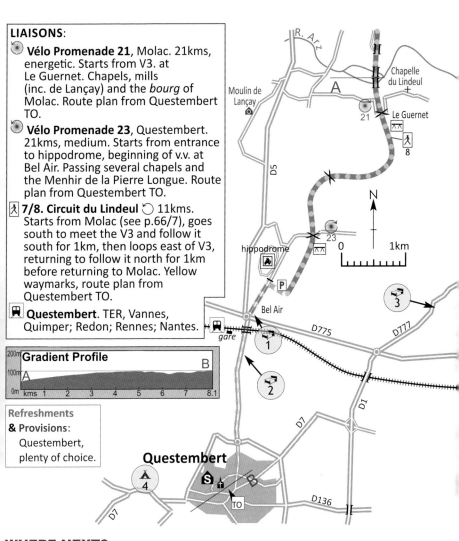

Gradient Profile

Refreshments & Provisions: Questembert, plenty of choice.

WHERE NEXT?

The V3, although named 'St-Malo to Rhuys', is now effectively behind you and although a map of cycle routes on the Presqu'île de Rhuys is available from Questembert TO, you are left to find your own way to the Rhuys peninsula. An interesting route would be via Le Gorvello, a pretty and lively village that straddles the border between the communes of Sulniac and Theix. Take the D7 south west from Questembert, through Berric and fork right (still with the D7) to Le Gorvello. From Le Gorvello go south to Surzur by the D183 (with a short detour to the fortified manor of Le Plessis Josso, open afternoons in July & August and the heritage weekend in September). From Surzur a minor road goes west to St-Armel where the Rhuys system of cycle routes (mostly on roads) offers a choice of directions. The Presqu'île de Rhuys has many attractions, not least of which is the Château de Suscinio (open all year except Christmas and New Year), and a fabulous coastline, especially overlooking the Gulf of Morbihan to the north.

The Reseau Breton to Camaret ran close to the south bank of the Nantes-Brest Canal between Port de Carhaix and Pont Triffen. This former railway has now been converted to Green Way as a marginally straighter alternative to the canal towpath, which is still the 'official' Green Way at this point. At Pont Triffen the old railway crossed the canal and continued on to Camaret on the Crozon peninsula. Since the V6 is still called Camaret to Vitré one can logically expect this Pont Trifffen - Port de Carhaix stretch to form part of the V6 when that route does eventually link up it's two extremities.

So, jumping the gun a little, it is here described from Pont Triffen to Carhaix as part of the V6 (temporarily, section number '0'). The route from Port de Carhaix to Carhaix-Plouguer shared with the V7 is included so as to link up with the rest of the V6.

Signage: universal cycle route signage - unspecific.

Route: ▶E from carpark at former Pont Triffen station (now *agri-coop* works) find start of Green Way to right of buildings. Follow for 11kms to car park at Port de Carhaix and here join the V7 northwards.

Surface: compacted sand, fair/good. Occasional tarmac.

Detours: alternative route offered by the canal towpath from Pont Triffen to Pont ar Brost, beyond Port de Carhaix.

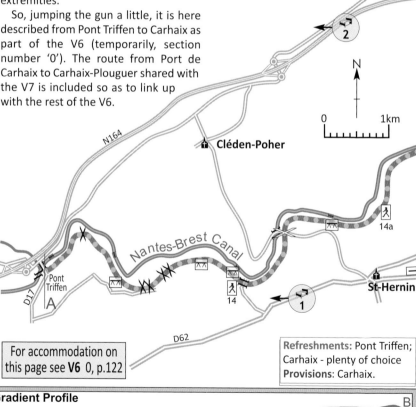

For accommodation on this page see **V6** 0, p.122

Refreshments: Pont Triffen; Carhaix - plenty of choice
Provisions: Carhaix.

200m **Gradient Profile**   B
100m A
0m kms 1   2   3   4   5   6   7   8   9   10 11 12 13 14 15 16 17 17.9

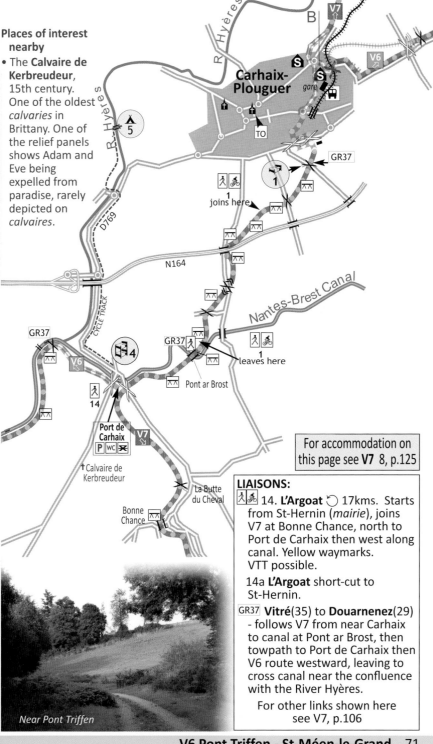

Places of interest nearby

- The **Calvaire de Kerbreudeur**, 15th century. One of the oldest *calvaries* in Brittany. One of the relief panels shows Adam and Eve being expelled from paradise, rarely depicted on *calvaries*.

R. Hyères

Carhaix-Plouguer *gare*

B

V7

V6

GR37

D769

N164

CYCLE TRACK

Nantes-Brest Canal

1 joins here

1 leaves here

GR37

GR37

V6

Pont ar Brost

Port de Carhaix P WC

V7

†Calvaire de Kerbreudeur

La Butte du Cheval

Bonne Chance

For accommodation on this page see **V7** 8, p.125

LIAISONS:

14. **L'Argoat** ○ 17kms. Starts from St-Hernin (*mairie*), joins V7 at Bonne Chance, north to Port de Carhaix then west along canal. Yellow waymarks. VTT possible.

14a **L'Argoat** short-cut to St-Hernin.

GR37 **Vitré**(35) to **Douarnenez**(29) - follows V7 from near Carhaix to canal at Pont ar Brost, then towpath to Port de Carhaix then V6 route westward, leaving to cross canal near the confluence with the River Hyères.

For other links shown here see V7, p.106

Near Pont Triffen

V6 1. **Carhaix to Maël-Carhaix** (11.9kms, roads + Green Way)
TO Carhaix 02 98 93 04 42 www.tourismecarhaix.poher.com
TO Rostrenen 02 96 29 02 72 www.tourismekreizbreizh.com

Starting out on the V6 from Carhaix one soon notices that it is different from the V7. After just a few metres of Green Way one is in the department of Côtes d'Armor. There is an absence of barriers, crossings being marked with just a STOP sign. The more elaborate signage includes kilometre posts and information panels to mark each detour (*balade à vélo*). These diversions based on the Green Way are waymarked with thin, white arrows on a dark green rectangle and they featured in a folder of route plans, *Balades à vélo autour de la voie verte du petit train* available from TOs in Côtes d'Armor. This may now be unavailable. The Maël-Carhaix / Le Moustoir detour affords an opportunity to find the Roman aqueduct that fed drinking water to Carhaix. It can be found again at a different point by following signs from Maël-Carhaix *bourg* (3kms).

Signage: ▶E - V6 Maël-Carhaix.
◀W - V6 Carhaix-Plouguer.

Route: ▶E **from Carhaix,** initially by road from the E.Leclerc roundabout (on V7 route). Exit roundabout as if to visit supermarket but continue, bearing left over level crossing, from where there is a cycle path on the left (not much used, apparently); follow it uphill, sharp left at T-junction, over hill, ahead over roundabout, take 1st left to Kervasdoué (village, not the industrial estate). In 200m turn right onto a former railway track-bed. Follow it to Maël-Carhaix.

Surface: compacted sand, fair/good.

Detours: see **Liaisons**

Entering Maël-Carhaix

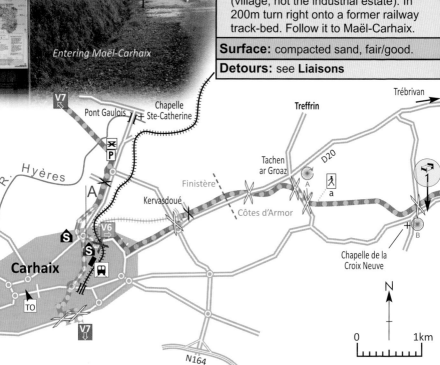

LIAISONS:

V7 **Roscoff to Concarneau**

A. Treffrin/Trébrivan circuit 15 kms easy. Start and return to V6 here, going via Treffrin, Pont Gaulois, Chapelle Ste-Catherine, Roman road, and Trébrivan. Waymarked clockwise - thin, white arrow on dark green rectangle.

B. Maël-Carhaix/Le Moustoir circuit 6kms easy. Goes via Chapelle de la Croix Neuve and Gallo-Roman aqueduct. Waymarked both ways - thin, white arrow on dark green rectangle.

(TOs - *Balades à vélo autour de la voie verte du petit train, Fiche 9*)

a. 'Hent Glas' circuit ↻ 14 kms, based on Treffrin and the V6. Yellow waymarks.

Carhaix TER trains to Guingamp.

Refreshments:
Carhaix - plenty of choice;
Tachen ar Groaz - bar/restaurant at crossroads;
Treffrin - bar/restaurant;
Maël-Carhaix - plenty of choice.
Provisions:
Carhaix - 2 supermarkets at junction V7/V6; Maël-Carhaix.

Places of interest nearby

- **Gallo-Roman aqueduct**, passing near Maël-Carhaix at Kervezennec.
- **Water garden** at Kervezennec, Maël-Carhaix. Public park, open all year.
- **Church of St-Hernin**, Locarn, with its wheel of fortune (bell-wheel).
- **Bois de Mezlé** (just south of Locarn) old slate workings. (short walk circuit).

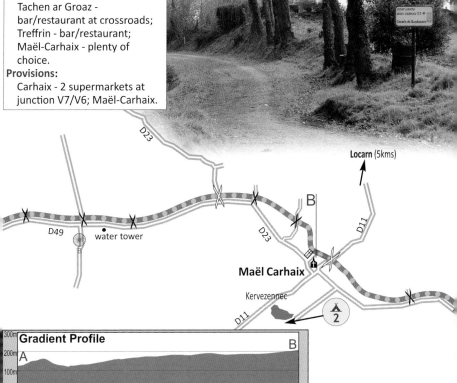

Locarn (5kms)

D23

B

D49   water tower   D23   D11

Maël Carhaix

Kervezennec

D11   ▲2

Gradient Profile

300m
200m A   B
100m
0m kms 1 2 3 4 5 6 7 8 9 10 11 11.9

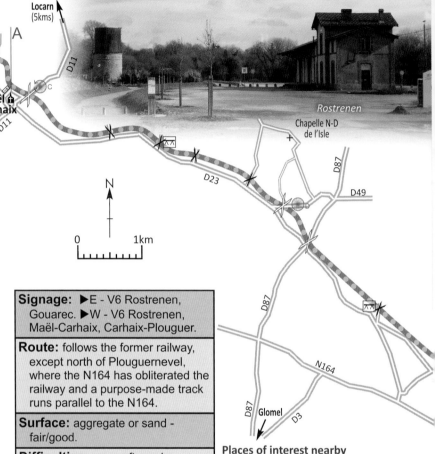

Signage: ▶E - V6 Rostrenen, Gouarec. ▶W - V6 Rostrenen, Maël-Carhaix, Carhaix-Plouguer.

Route: follows the former railway, except north of Plouguernevel, where the N164 has obliterated the railway and a purpose-made track runs parallel to the N164.

Surface: aggregate or sand - fair/good.

Difficulties: very soft sandy surface, especially between Rostrenen and Plouguernevel - drags on the tyres, especially when wet.

Detours: several family cycle rides into surrounding countryside provide access to places of interest (see Liaisons).

Places of interest nearby

- **Château de Coat Couravel** (5kms SW of Rostrenen, off D790) 14th century fortified house; gardens open all year.
- **Glomel** and the 'Grande Tranchée' on the Nantes-Brest canal.
- **Chapelle N-D de l'Isle**, 14th/17th century.
- **Manoir de Coaderneau**, Rostrenen (see Liaisons: ◉ F).

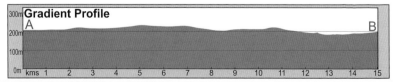

Gradient Profile

LIAISONS:

 c. Maël-Carhaix/Locarn 9.5 kms circuit, easy. Via the valley of the slate quarries, Locarn church and its wheel of fortune, then back through Maël-Carhaix to the watergardens of Kervezennec. Waymarked thin, white arrow on dark green rectangle.

d. Kergrist-Moëlou 14 kms circuit - easy. via Chapelle N-D de l'Isle, Calvaire de Kergrist, chapel & fontaine at St-Lubin. Waymarked either way thin, white arrow on dark green rectangle.

e. Rostrenen/Glomel 14 kms circuit - medium (some hills and earth paths). Chapelle Ste-Christine, Manoir de Coat-Couravel, Nantes-Brest Canal. Waymarked anti-clockwise thin, white arrow on dark. green rectangle.

(TOs - *Balades à vélo autour de la voie verte du petit train, Fiche 8*)

f. Rostrenen/Plouguernevel 4.5 kms circuit via Green Way, easy/medium (two hills). Via Manoir de Coaderneau. Waymarked either way thin, white arrow on dark. green rectangle.

(TOs - *Balades à vélo autour de la voie verte du petit train, Fiche 7*)

Refreshments: Maël-Carhaix, Rostrenen, Plouguernevel.
Provisions: Maël-Carhaix, Rostrenen (supermarkets, market day Tues), Plouguernevel.

Cycle ride information panel

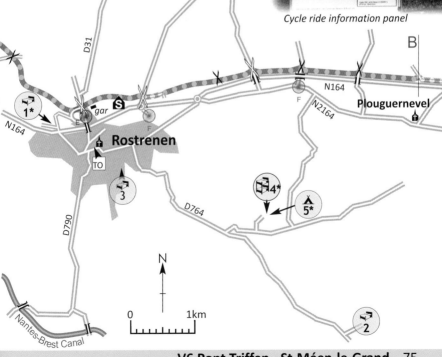

Abbaye de Bon Repos

Both Gouarec and Bon Repos make interesting stopping points. The former station at Gouarec is now a Tourist Office and *gîte d'étape*, while the town has some fine buildings, notably the Pavillon de Rohan, a former hunting lodge and now home to the AIKB (an English organisation which provides tourist information and helps expats integrate into French/Breton life).

Join the Nantes-Brest canal towpath for the next stretch of the V6 to Bon Repos. Here, a much visited former Cistercian abbey looks out over the canal. A popular attraction, there is always something going on during the summer and it's good for a refreshment break before climbing (on foot) to the Landes de Liscuis and its neolithic alley graves (*allées couvertes*).

N164 A
GR37
N2164
Plouguernevel

Chapelle St-Gilles
de Gouarec

GR37
b G

N164
2
Gouarec
V1

Nantes-Brest Canal
5 3*

Signage: ►E - V6 Gouarec, Caurel.
◄W - V6 Gouarec, Rostrenen.

Route: between Gouarec and Bon Repos the railway track-bed has been lost, so the V6 takes a detour via the Nantes/Brest canal towpath. After crossing Bon Repos bridge follow either V6 to Mur de Bretagne or V1 Velodyssey signed Pontivy: they rejoin after a couple of kilometres.

Surface: aggregate, fair. Some shared road.

Difficulties: west of Gouarec, the new N164 imposes a detour by a minor road and a new track steeply up and down to rejoin the line of the railway. Continuing on the road via the Chapelle St-Gilles de Gouarec is marginally easier and more interesting.
At Bon Repos, both routes to rejoin the railway involve a steep climb.

Detours: several opportunities to explore, by bike or on foot. Information on the ground is not lacking but is complex. See **Liaisons**.

LIAISONS:

🚲 6 **Circuit de Bon Repos** ↻ 36 km - VTT red. Starts at Station VTT at Base Départementale de Plein Air de Guerlédan. Via Bon Repos - Nantes-Brest canal - Beau Rivage on lake Guerlédan - Caurel wind-farm - St-Gelven *bourg*.

🚶 G. **Laniscat** 13 km circuit - easy. Starts by Rosquelfen chapel (if no signs from Gare de Gouarec, take main road R, fork L uphill to Rosquelfen). Via Landes de Liscuis, la loge Michel (slate house) Laniscat, Laniscat church. Waymarked thin, white arrow on dark green rectangle. (TOs - *Balades à vélo autour de la voie verte du petit train, Fiche 7*)

🚶 H. **Gouarec - Plélauff** 8 km circuit - easy/moderate. To Pléiauff and its unusual church bells, back via Nantes-Brest canal. Waymarked clockwise thin, white arrow on dark green rectangle. (TOs - *Balades à vélo autour de la voie verte du petit train, Fiche 7*)

🚶 I. **St-Gelven - Perret** 8 km circuit - easy. Via Les Forges des Salles and the forest of Quénécan. Waymarked clockwise thin, white arrow on dark green rectangle. (TOs - *Balades à vélo autour de la voie verte du petit train, Fiche 6*)

🚶 J. **St-Gelven** circuit, recently interrupted by road construction - follow waymarks, thin, white arrow on dark green rectangle. (TOs - *Balades à vélo autour de la voie verte du petit train, Fiche 6*)

continued on page 78

Gradient Profile

For **Places of Interest** see next page

Refreshments: Plouguernevel, Gouarec, Bon Repos (plenty of choice in season).
Provisions: Gouarec.

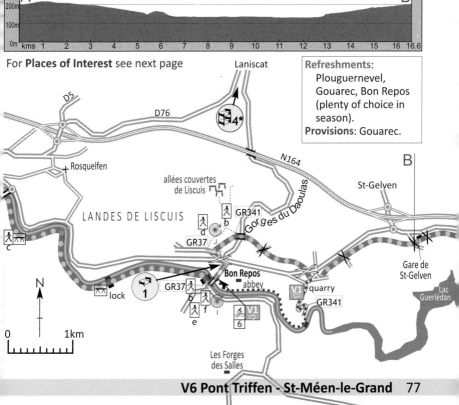

LIAISONS continued from p.77

`GR37` **Vitré to Douarnenez**. Arriving from the south east it has taken a slight diversion eastwards to reach Bon Repos, then leaves Bon Repos via the Landes de Liscuis. From Gouarec it continues westwards on the V6 as far as Plouguernevel.

`GR341` **Bréhec** (north coast) **to Riantec** (south coast). The GR341 arrives from the north via Laniscat to join the V6 at the Gorges du Daoulas and follow it eastwards to join the new route around Lac de Guerlédan (GR341N / GR341S. Caution: old and new routes in this area may have led to confused signage).

b. Landes de Liscuis circuit ↻12.5kms. Starts from Gouarec via Rosquelfen, Landes de Liscuis and alley graves, Bon Repos, Nantes-Brest canal (*Walks in Côtes d'Armor no.28 - Red Dog Books*).

c. Bois de Gouarec circuit ↺14kms. Starts at the Gare de Gouarec following V6 eastwards. Woodland walk up to old windmill tower and back to canal.

d. Landes de Liscuis circuit ↻ 11kms, starting at Rosquelfen by roads north of Landes de Liscuis, returning by part of outward route of b. (see above).

e. Bois de l'Abbaye circuit ↺ 6.5kms, starts on path between the canal and the Café de l'Abbaye.

f. Bois du Fao circuit ↻ 4.2kms. Starts on path opposite the abbey. Follow signs to Les Forges, then to La Croix Rouge, but at the road follow it R, back down to Bon Repos.

Pavillon de Rohan, Gouarec

Places of interest nearby

- **Chapelle St-Gilles de Gouarec**, formerly the parish church of Gouarec, hence it has an ossuary
- **Pavillon de Rohan**, Gouarec.
- **Loge Michel** - Route de Lann-Kergreis, Laniscat - a 19thC poor peasant's house, built entirely of local schist slabs and slate, and named after its last occupant,.
- **Abbey of Bon Repos** - Cistercian abbey founded in 1184 by Alain de Rohan, as a result of having a dream of the Virgin Mary whilst resting here after hunting. www.bon-repos.com
- **Les Forges des Salles** - well preserved 18th century iron-working village. www.lesforgesdessalles.info
- **Allées couvertes de Liscuis** - three Neolithic burial chambers.

Alley grave,
Landes de Liscuis

The Lac de Guerlédan is the largest lake in Brittany, formed in the first half of last century when the river Blavet was dammed for a hydro-electric project. The fact that the river Blavet was also the Nantes-Brest canal was by that time considered less important than the production of electricity. More than 80 years later the lake and its heavily wooded shores have become a leisure resort and prime tourist attraction. Holiday activity is centred around Beau Rivage (midway along the northern shore) and the Base Départementale de Plein Air de Guerlédan at the eastern end. The southern side is quieter with less habitation but consequently less accessible, although recently the GR341 footpath has been re-routed to go all round the lake, close to the water's edge. The Station VTT, situated at the Base de Plein Air, offers bike hire and 12 mountain bike circuits of varying difficulty (nos. 6 - 9 liaise with the V6) - route details with maps from the Station VTT and local TOs. For a shorter, gentler ride the *balade à vélo* ⦿ к Caurel will set the scene quite adequately. And remember, a canal and ten locks lie under those quiet waters.

Places of interest nearby

- **Coat Correc**, *allée couverte*.
- **Barrage de Guerlédan** and its electricity generating station, completed in 1930.
- **St-Aignan**, Musée de l'Electricité, - museum of electricity, inspired by the barrage de Guerlédan. Also, **St-Aignan church** is worth seeing.
- **Le Botrain**. Jardins du Botrain. Gardens around 18th century manor. Open Easter to Sept weekends, every day July/August, afternoon only (entrance fee). Menhir.
- **St-Guen**, Chapelle de St-Pabu. Dating from 1501 the chapel contains an imaginative carved rood-screen and part of a 16th century window.
- **Maison de Fendeur** (slate splitter's house) in the Bois de Caurel (see Liaisons 🚶 g. Bois de Caurel).
- **Base Départementale de Plein Air de Guerlédan** - an open air pursuits centre - rowing, canoeing, water-skiing, sailing, orienteering, climbing, trekking and hiking.

Chapelle de St-Pabu, St-Guen

- **Keriven**, a former slate working village.
- **Le Roz** (just north of St-Guen) - chapel, manor and a linen bleaching tank (*doué*).
- **Le Quillio** - church and *enclos paroissal*, cloth merchant's house.
- **Site de Lorette** - 289m hill near Le Quillio, megalithic site with chapel and elaborate fontaine nearby.

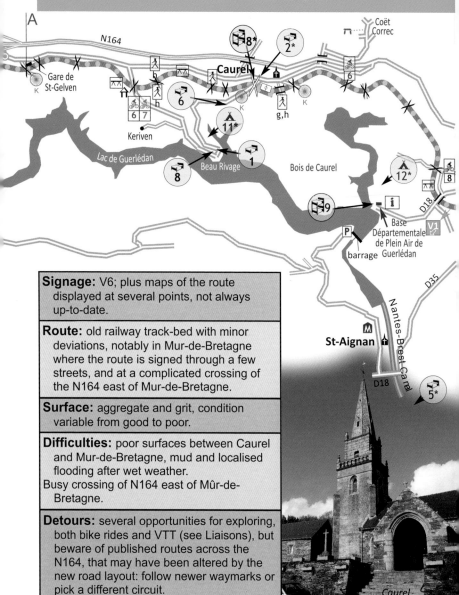

V6 4. St-Gelven to St-Guen

Signage: V6; plus maps of the route displayed at several points, not always up-to-date.

Route: old railway track-bed with minor deviations, notably in Mur-de-Bretagne where the route is signed through a few streets, and at a complicated crossing of the N164 east of Mur-de-Bretagne.

Surface: aggregate and grit, condition variable from good to poor.

Difficulties: poor surfaces between Caurel and Mur-de-Bretagne, mud and localised flooding after wet weather.
Busy crossing of N164 east of Mûr-de-Bretagne.

Detours: several opportunities for exploring, both bike rides and VTT (see Liaisons), but beware of published routes across the N164, that may have been altered by the new road layout: follow newer waymarks or pick a different circuit.

Gradient Profile

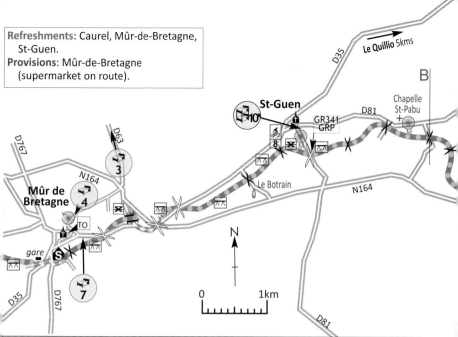

Refreshments: Caurel, Mûr-de-Bretagne, St-Guen.
Provisions: Mûr-de-Bretagne (supermarket on route).

LIAISONS:

Link to the V1, which follows the Nantes-Brest canal down to Pontivy. From there the V1 continues eastward along the Nantes-Brest canal and there is also a towpath along the Blavet down to Hennebont, near Lorient.

6 **Circuit de Bon Repos** ↺ 36 km - VTT red. Starts at Station VTT at Base Départementale de Plein Air de Guerlédan. Via Bon Repos - Nantes-Brest canal - Beau Rivage on lake Guerlédan - Caurel wind-farm - St-Gelven *bourg*.

7 **Circuit de Caurel** ↺ 20 km - VTT green. Starts at Station VTT at Base Départementale de Plein Air de Guerlédan. Via Caurel - Beau Rivage.

8 **Circuit de Lorette** ↺ 35 km circuit - VTT black. Starts at Station VTT at Base Départementale de Plein Air de Guerlédan. Via St-Guen - Le Quillio - St-Gilles-le-Vieux-Marché.

K **Caurel** 7.5 km circuit - easy. Starts at Caurel, westwards along V6 to Gare de St-Gelven, then down to Beau Rivage on the lake shore. Waymarked either way thin, white arrow on dark green rectangle.

L **Mûr-de-Bretagne** 10 km circuit - easy, but one steep descent. Via the valley of the Poullancre, St-Gilles-Vieux-Marché, Étang de la Martyre, Chapelle de N-D de Pitié de Bizidel. Waymarked thin, white arrow on dark green rectangle.

M **St-Guen - Le Quillio** 10 km circuit - easy, with some hills. Via linen bleaching tanks at Le Roz, the Cromlec'h de Lorette, Le Quillio *bourg*. Waymarked either way thin, white arrow on dark green rectangle.

GR341 **Bréhec** (north coast) to **Riantec** (south coast).

GRP **GRP de Pays des Toileux** (linen cloth country) long distance circuit.

g. **Bois de Caurel** circuit ↻ 8kms starting from sports field.

h. **Landes de Caurel** circuit ↺ 16kms starting from Caurel church, finishing on same route as g. but in opposite direction.

V6 5. St-Guen to Loudéac (17.2 kms, Green Way)
TO Mûr-de-Bretagne 02 96 28 51 41 www.guerledan.fr
TO Loudéac 02 96 28 25 17 www.centrebretagne.com

The Rigole d'Hilvern is the highlight of this section of the Green Way. A 63.5km feeder channel carrying water from the river Oust at Bosméléac to Hilvern, the highest point of the Nantes-Brest canal between the Oust and Blavet valleys. The rigole was dug entirely by hand between 1828 and 1838, following the lie of the land with a fall of 3cm per 100 metres. The trench was lined with clay, reinforced by stonework at vulnerable points, because when it was first filled with water it leaked like a sieve. It can be cycled in either direction from here, southwards as far as Hémonstoir (12kms) or northwards, where it's route now forms part of the V8 St-Brieuc to Lorient

Signage: V6, plus occasional maps of the route.

Route: former railway track-bed from St-Guen to river Oust at St-Caradec, after which the line is lost until about 2km before Loudéac. V6 signed on roads through Loudéac.

Surface: aggregate and grit, fair to good.

Difficulties: tortuous negotiation of new major road junction west of Loudéac.
Kerb not lowered at end of Green Way entering Loudéac from the west.

Detours: see Liaisons.

Chapelle St-Laurent

Places of interest nearby
- **Rigole d'Hilvern** (see map).
- **Chapelle St-Laurent** (see map).
- **St-Thélo**: several linen merchants' houses, one of which is now a museum of the industry.
- **Hémonstoir**: church and nearby three fountains (*trois fontaines*) 12th/13th century.

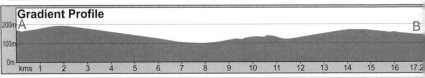

Gradient Profile

LIAISONS:

V8 St-Brieuc to Lorient - see p.115 (Rigole Green Way continues to Hémonstoir)

9 **Circuit de la Rigole d'Hilvern** ↻ 37 kms - VTT. Starts at Uzel (Station VTT) via Le Quillio - St-Guen - the V6 - the Rigole d'Hilvern - St-Thélo. www.base-plein-air-guerledan.com - route map from TO Mûr de Bretagne.

N **St-Caradec/St-Thélo** 13 km circuit - moderate. Via Rigole d'Hilvern, St-Thélo, St-Caradec, and along the V6. Waymarked either way thin, white arrow on dark green rectangle. (TOs - *Balades à vélo autour de la voie verte du petit train, Fiche 4*)

O **St-Caradec/Hémonstoir** 10km circuit, energetic. Waymarked same as N. (TOs - *Balades à vélo autour de la voie verte du petit train, Fiche 4*)

i. **Au fil de la Rigole d'Hilvern** circuit ↻15kms, starting from St-Caradec church, crossing V6 via the Rigole d'Hilvern, which it follows to Hémonstoir, meeting the V6 again on return to St-Caradec. Yellow waymarks.

GR341 **Bréhec** (north coast) to **Riantec** (south coast). Coming from the north it follows the V6 eastwards from St-Guen, leaves it north again to find the Rigole d'Hilvern, then follows that south.

GRP **GRP de Pays des Toileux** (linen cloth country) long distance circuit.

Buses only from Loudéac station, no train service.

Refreshments / Provisions: St-Caradec and Loudéac.

Rigole d'Hilvern

Continuing east, the Green Way misses Loudéac forest but makes up for it later with some pleasantly wild river scenery. At Pont Querra on the Lié, the local community of communes has built a 'Bases Sports Nature' including a watersports centre for canoeing and kayaking, and a 'Station VTT' for mountain bikers. The latter has a bike washing facility, bike hire and a leaflet of the various VTT circuits.

Signage: V6; Chemin de Randonnée
▶E - La Prénessaye, Laurenan.
◀W - La Prénessaye, Loudéac

Route: mostly former railway track-bed - easy to follow.

Surface: aggregate and grit, mostly good.

Difficulties: St-Lubin quarry - heavy plant crossing and a steep slope.

Detours: Querrien (⇆7.5kms) see Places of interest nearby (included in wider circuits - see liaisons).

LIAISONS:

1 Circuit du Minerai ↺ 24 or 27 km - VTT blue. Start: Pont Querra via V6 southwest to N164, then east via Plémet to Réneac, north to Launay Guen (see next page). From there, 1B returns on V6. to Pont Querra, 1A takes a detour north.

2 Circuit de Querrien ↻ 13 km - VTT green. Starts at Pont Querra, via Querrien to V6 near St-Lubin gare and returns along V6.

P Loudéac to Loudéac Forest 5km direct, easy. Waymarked thin, white arrow on dark green rectangle. From St-Guillaume (on edge of forest) two red VTT circuits go ↺ through the forest - no.11 (25km) & no.12 (32km).

Q La Chèze 10.5km circuit - easy. Waymarked either way thin, white arrow on dark green rectangle.

R Plémet/La Prénessaye 8km circuit - hilly. Via Querrien. Waymarked either way thin, white arrow on dark green rectangle.

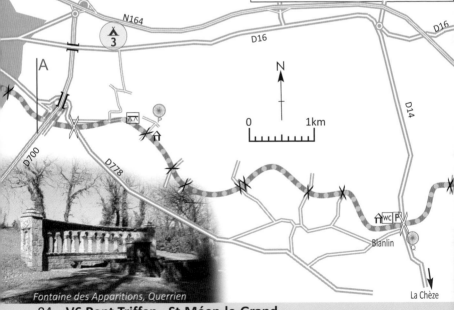

Fontaine des Apparitions, Querrien

s Plémet/Le Vaublanc 5km circuit - easy but hilly. Via the old iron-working site at Le Vaublanc. Waymarked thin, white arrow on dark green rectangle. (NB. the marker panel at this point may be incorrect and refer to the Plémet/La Prénessaye circuit.)

GRP Circuit du Petit Méné comes from Merdrignac to here via V6 (with a loop south to Goméné) and leaves from here to link with the GRP Pays des Toileux (see p.81, 83 & 116)

j. Marche vers Querrien circuit ↻ 24kms (short-cut 16.3kms), medium. Starts at Pont Querra via V6 eastwards, St-Lubin (chapel), Fontaine des Apparitions and Chapelle N-D-de-Toute-Aide at Querrien, La Prénessaye. Yellow waymarks.

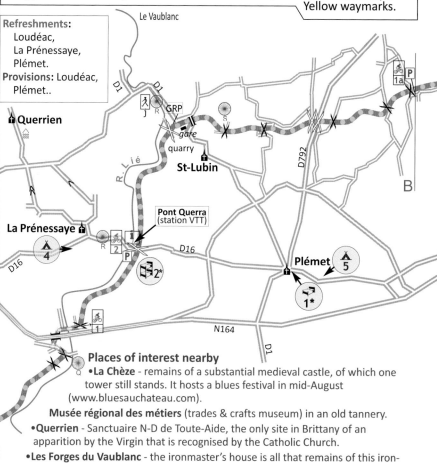

Refreshments:
  Loudéac,
  La Prénessaye,
  Plémet.
Provisions: Loudéac,
  Plémet..

Le Vaublanc

Querrien

GRP

gare

quarry

St-Lubin

B

La Prénessaye

Pont Querra
(station VTT)

D16

Plémet

N164

Places of interest nearby

- **La Chèze** - remains of a substantial medieval castle, of which one tower still stands. It hosts a blues festival in mid-August (www.bluesauchateau.com).

  Musée régional des métiers (trades & crafts museum) in an old tannery.

- **Querrien** - Sanctuaire N-D de Toute-Aide, the only site in Brittany of an apparition by the Virgin that is recognised by the Catholic Church.

- **Les Forges du Vaublanc** - the ironmaster's house is all that remains of this iron-working site, which operated from 1671 to 1880, using local ore, charcoal from Loudéac forest and power from the river Lié.

Gradient Profile

A

B

kms 1 2 3 4 5 6 7 8 9 10 11 12 13 14 15 16 17 18.6

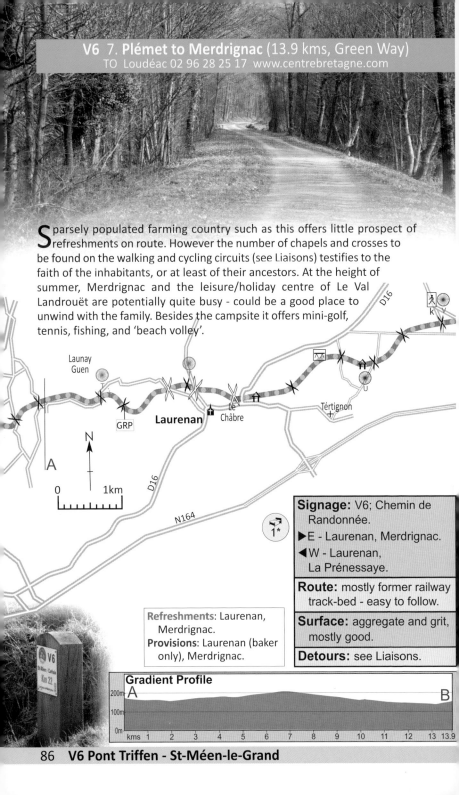

Sparsely populated farming country such as this offers little prospect of refreshments on route. However the number of chapels and crosses to be found on the walking and cycling circuits (see Liaisons) testifies to the faith of the inhabitants, or at least of their ancestors. At the height of summer, Merdrignac and the leisure/holiday centre of Le Val Landrouët are potentially quite busy - could be a good place to unwind with the family. Besides the campsite it offers mini-golf, tennis, fishing, and 'beach volley'.

Signage: V6; Chemin de Randonnée.
▶E - Laurenan, Merdrignac.
◀W - Laurenan, La Prénessaye.

Route: mostly former railway track-bed - easy to follow.

Surface: aggregate and grit, mostly good.

Detours: see Liaisons.

Refreshments: Laurenan, Merdrignac.
Provisions: Laurenan (baker only), Merdrignac.

Gradient Profile

Le Val Landrouët, Merdrignac

Places of interest nearby

- **Chemin d'Estrat**, the Roman road from Corseul (*Fanum Martis*) to Vannes (*Darioritum*) approaches Laurenan from the north east. See Liaisons 🚶 k.
- **Laurenan**. Stone cross, 12th/13th century, next to car park behind the church.

Chapelle St-Yves, Tértignon

LIAISONS:

т Laurenan
6.5km circuit - easy, some earth paths. To the Chapelle St-Unet (re-built 1879). Waymarked thin, white arrow on dark green rectangle.

u Goméné 16.5km circuit - medium, two steep hills. Via Chapelle St-Yves at Tértignon, Chapelle Ste-Anne at Roquetton, three crosses at Le Tertre Feuillet, Goméné *bourg*, St-Guénaël, chapel and cross. Waymarked either way thin, white arrow on dark green rectangle.

v St-Vran 5km circuit - medium, hills and earth paths. Via Chapelle St-Lambert. Waymarked either way thin, white arrow on dark green rectangle.

w Le train de la balade 18km circuit - easy. Same route as 🚶 l (see below), VTT22 waymarks.

GRP Circuit du Petit Méné, which runs along V6 from Merdrignac to St-Lubin (see p.85), here takes an optional detour south to Goméné.

🚶 **k. Aux carrefours des voies** (short-cut) circuit ↻ 10.5kms . Starts at Laurenan via V6 eastwards, returns to Laurenan via Roman road. Yellow waymarks. (*Walks in Côtes d'Armor* no.22 - Red Dog Books)

🚶 **l. Le train de la balade** circuit ↻ 18kms. Starts at Val de Landrouët (on V6 at Merdrignac, to Goméné (detour to Menhir de Pellionaye) and Chapelle St-Guénaël. Returns eastwards along V6 to Merdrignac. VTT22 waymarks.

V6 8. **Merdrignac to Trémorel** (11.6 kms, Green Way)
TO Loudéac 02 96 28 25 17 www.centrebretagne.com
Merdrignac 02 96 28 47 98

Around Trémorel and to the east, older houses built of earth become more and more common. This is the geological area of the Rennes basin where stone is scarce. Mud and straw were built up in layers between wooden shuttering, the layers usually remaining visible in the finished wall. A few examples of this method remain in the centre of Trémorel, others are dotted around the countryside, one right by the V6 about 1km east of the N164 crossing.

Signage: V6; Chemin de Randonnée
▶E - Trémorel, St-Méen-le-Grand.
◀W - Merdrignac.

Route: mostly former railway track-bed - easy to follow.

Surface: aggregate and grit, mostly good.

Difficulties: surface occasionally washed away by floods - makes a bumpy ride.

Detours: from Trémorel take the D52 north to see the chapel of 13 oak trees. Lord and Lady Ben Brook (18th century) planted an oak for each of their 13 children.

Trémorel

LIAISONS:

❋ x **Merdrignac** 10.5km circuit - easy. Via Chapelle Ste-Philomène and Chapelle St-Brieuc des Bois. Waymarked either way thin, white arrow on dark green rectangle. (Note: the information panel at the eastern intersection with the V6 has the 'you are here' arrow in quite the wrong position - unless it has been corrected recently.)

❋ Y **De clochers en chapelles** (from church towers to chapels) 45km - easy. Start: Merdrignac, 3kms on V6 eastwards then south via St-Brieuc-des-Bois, Chapelle Ste-Philomène, Chapelle St-Yves, Illifaut, Loscouët-sur-Meu, returning to V6 beyond Trémorel. Yellow waymarks to Chapelle St-Yves, then wooden panels *'De clochers en chapelles'.*

❋ z **Loscouët-sur-Meu** 4.5km circuit - easy. Via fishing lake (*centre Européen de pêche de Spécimens*), Le Pont des Portes (look for statue of St-Lunaire under the bridge - the source at his feet cures eye ailments), church of St-Lunaire at Loscouët. Waymarked either way thin, white arrow on dark green rectangle. (Possible link to V3 - see p.57 Detours.)

Looks peaceful enough...

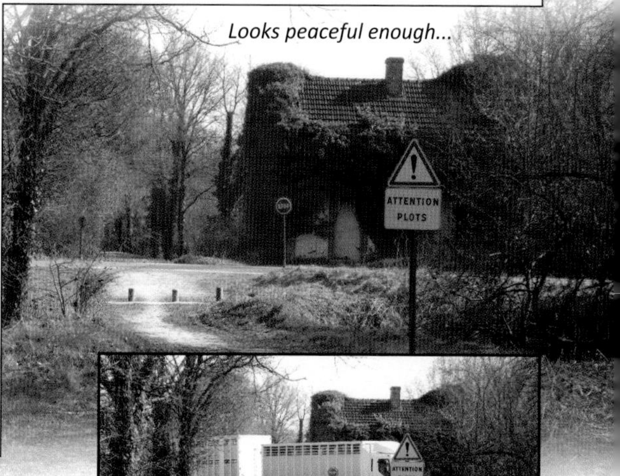

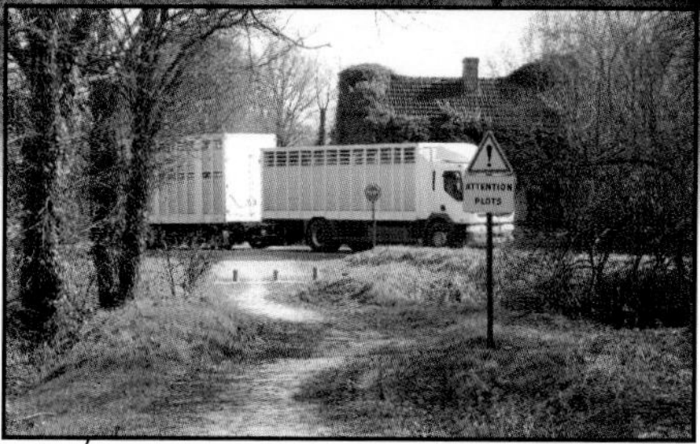

...but take care!

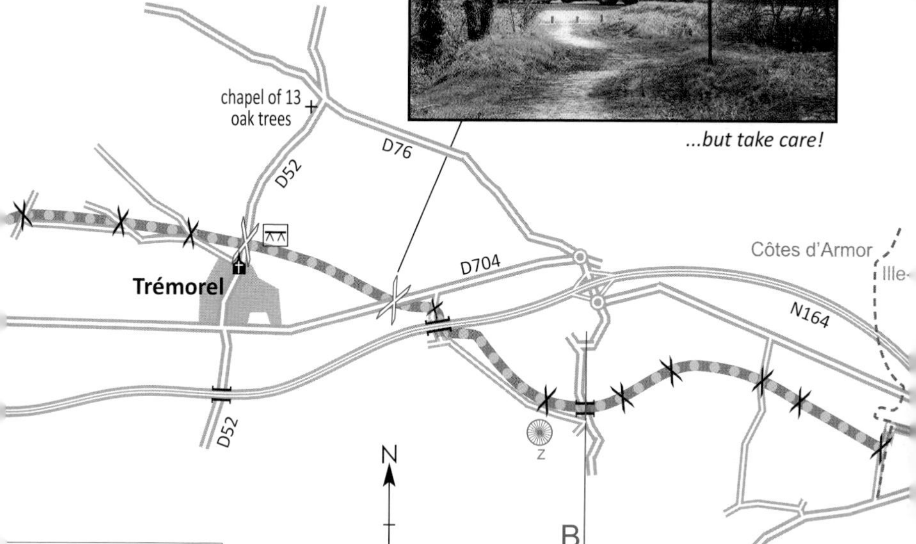

chapel of 13 oak trees

D52

D76

D704

Trémorel

Côtes d'Armor

Ille-

N164

D52

N

z

B

Refreshments: Trémorel.
Provisions: Trémorel.

0   1km

From the end of the Green Way at Beauregard there is just a further 3kms on a fairly quiet road route into St-Méen-le-Grand. A pleasant if unremarkable town centre (except for the sugarloaf *mairie*) but the *Abbatiale* (abbey church) is worth seeing - guided visits are arranged by the Tourist Office.

For cycling afficionados the Tourist Office shares its building with a museum dedicated to the career of Louison Bobet, professional cyclist from 1947 to 1962, clocking up 122 victories. He was a native of St-Méen.

Signage: ▶E - V6 St-Méen-le-Grand.
▶W - V6 Carhaix

Route: former railway track-bed as far as departmental boundary, then signed road route to outskirts of St-Méen.

Surface: compacted sand fair/good. Road route tarmac, variable.

Detours: see Liaisons: ⊚ z provides a link to the V3 southwards.
From Loscouët-sur-Meu follow signs to Gaël (see p.57 Detours).

Refreshments: St-Méen-le-Grand, plenty of choice.
Provisions: St-Méen-le-Grand.

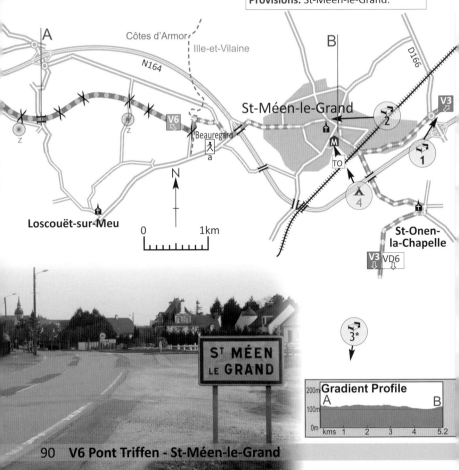

St-Méen-le-Grand

LIAISONS:

⊙ z **Loscouët-sur-Meu** 4.5km circuit - easy. Via fishing lake (*centre Européen de pêche de Spécimens*), Le Pont des Portes (look for statue of St-Lunaire under the bridge - the source at his feet cures eye ailments), church of St-Lunaire at Loscouët. Waymarked either way, thin, white arrow on dark green rectangle. (Possible link to V3 - see Detours)

🚶 **m. Circuit du Beauregard** ↻ 6kms. Starts at Beauregard and follows part of the old Roman road (*chemin des moines* - the monks' road) to Paimpont and the forest of Brocéliande.

V3 **St-Malo to Rhuys**. ▶N - St-Malo: road route (signed) to the D220 at Médréac then mostly Green Way to Dinard for St-Malo. ▶S - Rhuys via Questembert: road route (signed) to St-Léry, then Green Way to Questembert.

VD6 **St-Méen to Vitré**. Road route (signed) to the Green Way near Moutiers, then following the Green Way to Vitré.

Places of interest nearby

- **St-Méen-le-Grand**: elements of the Abbatiale date from the 11th century. Guided visits arranged by the Tourist Office.
- **Musée Louison Bobet** in the same building as the Tourist Office.

WHERE NEXT?

The centre of St-Méen-le-Grand appears to have been kept free of signage for cycle routes, leaving one with a sense of having been brought here and then abandoned. However, follow signs to St-Onen-La-Chapelle and, 50m after crossing the railway, the cycle route signs re-appear where the road forks. This is where the V3 touches St-Méen at the half-way stage of its road route from Médréac to St-Léry (see p.54-57) - left fork to Médréac, right fork to St-Léry.

Having arrived on the V6 from Carhaix, one can either follow the V3, north to St-Malo or south as far as Questembert, or continue eastwards on the Ille-et-Vilaine cycle route VD6 that eventually arrives at Vitré, via the Green Way from Moutiers. If opting for the VD6, set off initially on the V3 southwards (see p.56), direction St-Onen-la-Chapelle. A few kilometres after St-Onen the VD6 continues ahead (signed Muël) where the V3 goes right.

V7 1. Roscoff to Lanvéguen (12kms, mostly by road)

TO Roscoff 02 98 61 12 13 www.roscoff-tourisme.com
St Pol-de-Léon 02 98 69 05 69 http://www.saintpoldeleon.fr

For the first few kilometres the V7 cycle route follows the east coast of the Roscoff peninsular, with views across the Bay of Morlaix. Once past St-Pol-de-Léon, one is looking across the Penzé estuary towards Carantec and the Île de Callot (a former Viking stronghold). Finally the Pont de la Corde road bridge comes into view before the cycle-route strikes inland to Lanvéguen.

This area is the Pays de Léon, famous for its vegetables. Fields of artichokes, cauliflowers, and onions are a common sight. Brittany Ferries was founded in 1972, initially to take vegetables to Plymouth for the English market; passengers with cars (and bicycles without onions) came later.

Places of interest nearby

- **Roscoff**, 'Petite Cité de Caractère' built with the wealth of successful merchants and ship owners.
  A museum is dedicated to the 'Johnnies', the onion-sellers who took ship for England, their bikes festooned with *oignons roses*, the pink onions that are still a speciality of this region.
- **St-Pol-de-Léon**. The church, (formerly a cathedral when Léon was a diocese), is dedicated to St-Pol Aurélien, one of the seven founding saints of Brittany.

Signage:
- ▶S - V7 St-Pol-de-Léon, Morlaix.
- ▶N - V7 St-Pol-de-Léon, Roscoff.

V7 not signed in St-Pol centre; follow road signs to Morlaix (▶S) or Roscoff (▶N).

Route: Velodyssey, Tour de Manche and the V7 all share the same route here.

- ▶S - turn left from ferry port at Roscoff, cross railway, turn left immediately on stony track. Follow V7 signage via minor roads, arriving in St-Pol-de-Léon by the water tower. Follow road signs to Morlaix through St-Pol, turning left by Chapelle du Kreisker (tall spire), then right at roundabout where cycle signage restarts. Follow for 5km. After Tréver, look for V7 sign left. Follow signed route, across main road and up to Lanvéguen.
- ▶N - Over level-crossing continue ahead on track following V7 signs to St-Pol. Here follow Roscoff road signs. Past cathedral take broad *pavé* street uphill, but turn right and bear left around parking area. Continue up towards water tower to find V7 route signed to Roscoff.

Surface: mostly tarmac, occasional stony tracks and earth paths, pavé in St-Pol.

Difficulties: Hilly route Roscoff to St-Pol. Hill up to Lanvéguen.

Gradient Profile

100m | A | | | | | | | | | | | | B
0m | kms | 1 | 2 | 3 | 4 | 5 | 6 | 7 | 8 | 9 | 10 | 11 | 12

Roscoff

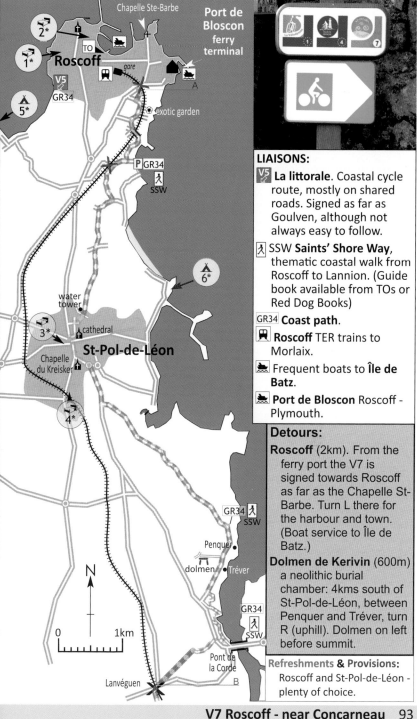

Chapelle Ste-Barbe

Port de Bloscon ferry terminal

Roscoff

TO

gare

V5
GR34

exotic garden

P GR34
SSW

water tower

cathedral

St-Pol-de-Léon

Chapelle du Kreisker

N

0   1km

Penquer
dolmen   Tréver

GR34
SSW

GR34
SSW

Pont de la Corde

Lanvéguen

A

B

LIAISONS:

V5 **La littorale**. Coastal cycle route, mostly on shared roads. Signed as far as Goulven, although not always easy to follow.

SSW **Saints' Shore Way**, thematic coastal walk from Roscoff to Lannion. (Guide book available from TOs or Red Dog Books)

GR34 **Coast path**.

Roscoff TER trains to Morlaix.

Frequent boats to **Île de Batz**.

Port de Bloscon Roscoff - Plymouth.

Detours:

Roscoff (2km). From the ferry port the V7 is signed towards Roscoff as far as the Chapelle St-Barbe. Turn L there for the harbour and town. (Boat service to Île de Batz.)

Dolmen de Kerivin (600m) a neolithic burial chamber: 4kms south of St-Pol-de-Léon, between Penquer and Tréver, turn R (uphill). Dolmen on left before summit.

Refreshments & Provisions:
Roscoff and St-Pol-de-Léon - plenty of choice.

An easy ride downhill to the river Penzé, where an impressive viaduct carries the Roscoff to Morlaix railway over the valley. From here the road follows the river bank to cross over at the village of Penzé. After leaving Penzé the route is mostly quiet roads through farmland and forest, over the railway and the main road to Roscoff (D58) then up to the high ground above Morlaix before dropping down to the Morlaix river and town centre.

Refreshments: at Kerlaudy, Penzé and Taulé (1km).
Provisions: Taulé, or Géant in Morlaix For a big sports shop, including cycling gear and gadgets, it's an easy detour to Decathlon on the way in to Morlaix.

Signage: ▶S - V7 Morlaix. ▶N - St-Pol-de-Léon.

Route: At Lanvéguen, cross railway and bear left on D769 downhill to follow road beside river Penzé. At Penzé village, cross river and continue ahead. At fork in the village, the D119 (not marked) to the left offers an initial steep climb but is quieter than the signed V7 route via D769 and without the blind bends. Where D119 crosses D769 continue on D119. Continue ahead at all junctions, over level crossing and down to roundabout. Turn left over bridge, over another roundabout then left uphill to cycle track on right. The road opposite the far end of the cycle track offers an easy downhill alternative to much of the V7 signed route through suburbs and avoids a footbridge (with steps) over the N12.

Surface: mostly tarmac roads, variable.

Difficulties: ▶S out of Penzé, choice of the signed route by D769, uphill with blind bends, or quieter D119 with initial steep hill.
Footbridge over N12 on signed V7, but see map for road alternative.

Detours: (⇆5km) to ruined **Château de Penhoat**. In Penzé, don't take alternative route left but continue on D769, shortly to turn right on minor road. Cross over D19, then at a mill on left, follow road right 150m to car park. Short footpath to château ruins. Return to Penzé or follow D19 to Morlaix (busy road).

Places of interest nearby

- Château de Penhoat (see Detours). This 13th century castle occupies a promontory at the confluence of the rivers Penzé and Coatoulzac'h, overlooking the old road from Morlaix to Lesneven. The lords of Penhoat held lands extending over eight parishes, including many farms and three mills near the château as well as fisheries and a dovecote. They had the right to dispense justice, which would have been advertised by a gallows of four posts.

Three elements of the castle are discernable today: the central enclosure flanked by towers at the angles; the lodgings built against the inside of the curtain walls; and a bailey that sheltered the local population in times of trouble. The whole is surrounded by an impressive dry moat and an outer bank.

In summer, a local association organises medieval festivals and guided visits.

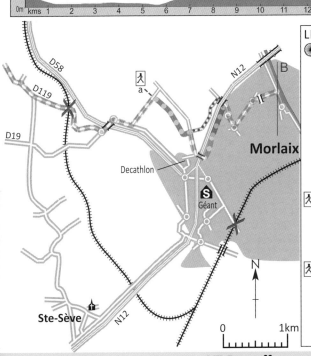

LIAISONS:

1. **La Boucle Léonarde** has followed the V7 from Roscoff and here leaves it to cut across the peninsula to Port Neuf (near Sibiril), then follow the V5 La Littorale back to Roscoff.

3. **Les deux vallées** ↻ 22.5km. Starts in Taulé and passes Château de Penhoat

a **La Vallée de la Pennélé** ↻ 10.5km, medium. Starts at Morlaix harbour (near point B)

What the cyclist needs to know about Morlaix is that its centre lies in a deep valley while its outskirts spread over the surrounding hills. That's fine when cycling into Morlaix but not so good when leaving. There is no officially recommended cycle route through Morlaix; the suggested route on the map is merely what seems the best option. Strategically placed street furniture near the Hotel de Ville (see picture below) will enable you to secure your bike while you explore Morlaix on foot.

Pedestrian access through first level of the viaduct

Market day is Saturday, with an all-day market between the viaduct and the hôtel de ville and a morning food market in the square (Place Allende) at the top of Grand'Rue.

Places of interest nearby
- A visit to the Tourist Office is recommended to pick up a plan of the town showing all its attractions - and there are many. Don't miss Grand'Rue, a street of half timbered, jettied houses, originally belonging to nobles who gave up their castles to become merchants. No.9 Grand' Rue is open to the public and illustrates the interior design, peculiar to Morlaix, whereby all the rooms are accessed from a central hall and staircase, with galleries (*pondalez*) linking the front and rear of the building.

Cycle rack near Hotel de Ville

Refreshments: Morlaix, plenty of choice.
Provisions: Géant (p.95) or central Morlaix. (Saturday morning market, Place Allende.)

Signage: ▶S Morlaix, Carhaix.
Morlaix centre is unsigned for cyclists, but a sign is placed to catch the eye of cyclists as they leave the *Maison de Randonnée* and guide them through back streets to the V7 southwards.
▶N St-Pol-de-Léon, Roscoff.

Route: ▶S at 'A' turn right, and continue ahead over roundabout keeping harbour on your left. At large roundabout continue ahead, under viaduct, past Hotel de Ville on left (stop here to park bike and explore town centre). At traffic lights go left. At T-junction go right. At traffic lights go left. (Beyond car park, now on right, is town museum in former convent, *Couvent des Jacobins*). Follow road right and uphill, rue des Vignes, and continue uphill on rue de Bréhat. At top the Green Way leaves on the right, along former railway (look left for old bridge, almost filled in).

Surface: tarmac, occasionally *pavé*.

Difficulties: ▶S no cycle route signs in central Morlaix. Steep hill up to point B.
▶N the left turn at point A is unsigned.

Detours: Morlaix town centre - well worth stopping a while.

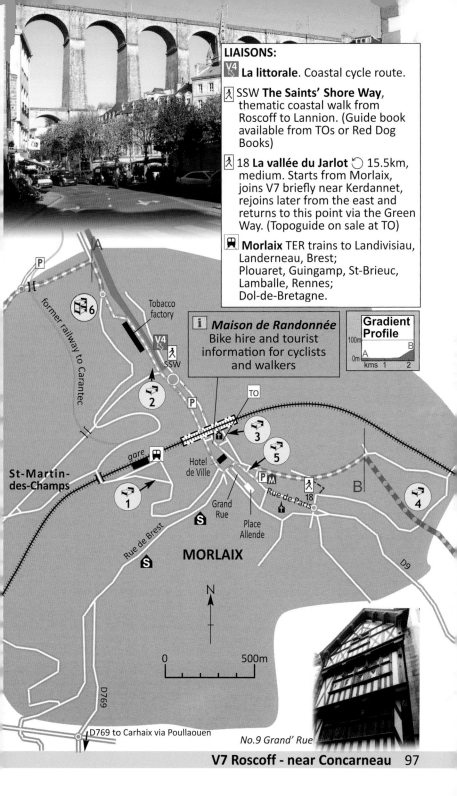

LIAISONS:

V4 **La littorale**. Coastal cycle route.

SSW **The Saints' Shore Way**, thematic coastal walk from Roscoff to Lannion. (Guide book available from TOs or Red Dog Books)

18 **La vallée du Jarlot** ↻ 15.5km, medium. Starts from Morlaix, joins V7 briefly near Kerdannet, rejoins later from the east and returns to this point via the Green Way. (Topoguide on sale at TO)

Morlaix TER trains to Landivisiau, Landerneau, Brest; Plouaret, Guingamp, St-Brieuc, Lamballe, Rennes; Dol-de-Bretagne.

former railway to Carantec

Tobacco factory

V4

SSW

i *Maison de Randonnée* Bike hire and tourist information for cyclists and walkers

Gradient Profile

100m

A B

0m

kms 1 2

TO

gare

St-Martin-des-Champs

Hotel de Ville

Grand Rue

Place Allende

Rue de Paris

18

Rue de Brest

MORLAIX

N

D9

0 500m

D769

D769 to Carhaix via Poullaouen

No.9 Grand' Rue

V7 4. Morlaix to Coatélan (8.3kms, Green Way)
TO Morlaix 02 98 62 14 94 www.tourisme.morlaix.fr

This is the beginning of the Green Way system based upon on the Réseau Breton (Breton network), the old metre gauge railway that crossed Brittany from east to west and north to south. The Morlaix to Carhaix section was the first to be opened, on 28th September 1891, so it's appropriate to start here.

The first part of this section leaves the suburbia of Morlaix and after crossing the D9 passes quietly under a canopy of trees along impressive embankments or through deep cuttings. Approaching Coetélan it becomes more open, crossed by many farm tracks, each with its barriers to prevent motorised traffic using the Green Way. The barriers can be an obstacle for cyclists when the gap is too narrow, and these in north Finistère are particularly bothersome.

Signage: ▶S - V7 Pont Noir, Gare de Scrignac, Poullaouen, Carhaix.
▶N - V7 Pont Noir, Morlaix.

Route: former railway track-bed all the way - easy to follow, except at Pont Noir where the embankment has been removed in straightening the D9 - follow through picnic area to cross over D9 and continue on the Green Way.

Surface: ▶S compacted sand (fair to good), initially stony as far as Pont Noir.

Difficulties: three busy road crossings. Narrowness of the surfaced path from Morlaix to Pont Noir. Many barriers with narrow openings.

Gradient Profile

The start of the Green Way.

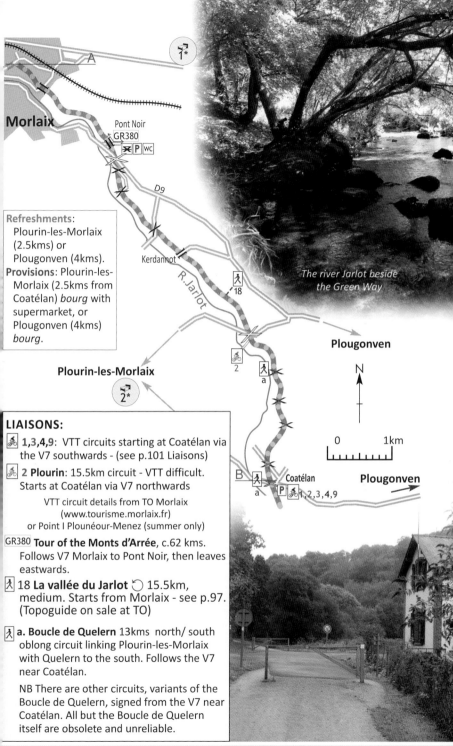

Morlaix

Pont Noir
GR380
✕ P wc

A

↱1

D9

Kerdannot

R. Jarlot

🚶18

The river Jarlot beside
the Green Way

Plougonven

Refreshments:
 Plourin-les-Morlaix
 (2.5kms) or
 Plougonven (4kms).
Provisions: Plourin-les-
 Morlaix (2.5kms from
 Coatélan) *bourg* with
 supermarket, or
 Plougonven (4kms)
 bourg.

Plourin-les-Morlaix

↱2*

🚲2

🚶a

N

0   1km

B 🚶
a P 🚲1,2,3,4,9

Coatélan

Plougonven ➤

LIAISONS:

🚲 **1,3,4,9**: VTT circuits starting at Coatélan via
the V7 southwards - (see p.101 Liaisons)

🚲 **2 Plourin**: 15.5km circuit - VTT difficult.
Starts at Coatélan via V7 northwards

> VTT circuit details from TO Morlaix
> (www.tourisme.morlaix.fr)
> or Point I Plounéour-Menez (summer only)

GR380 **Tour of the Monts d'Arrée**, c.62 kms.
Follows V7 Morlaix to Pont Noir, then leaves
eastwards.

🚶 18 **La vallée du Jarlot** ↻ 15.5km,
medium. Starts from Morlaix - see p.97.
(Topoguide on sale at TO)

🚶 **a. Boucle de Quelern** 13kms north/ south
oblong circuit linking Plourin-les-Morlaix
with Quelern to the south. Follows the V7
near Coatélan.

NB There are other circuits, variants of the
Boucle de Quelern, signed from the V7 near
Coatélan. All but the Boucle de Quelern
itself are obsolete and unreliable.

There is no avoiding this steady climb over the Monts d'Arrée, the highest hills in Brittany, but for compensation this is considered by many to be the most scenic section of the network. It divides into two halves - the climb from Coatélan to the Gare de Kermeur, then the descent to the Gare de Scrignac. A few little forays (see Detours) into the surrounding countryside are suggested to find various points of interest, such as the Wolf Museum at Cloître St-Thégonnec, the two menhirs near Kermeur or the Chapel of St-Corentin at Trinivel. The best of the scenery, however, can be found on the VTT circuits, especially nos.4 and 7.

Places of interest nearby

- **Wolf Museum** (Musée du Loup), Le Cloître St-Thégonnec. Open Sunday pm mid-Feb to mid-Dec, every afternoon in July and August (see Detours).
- **Two menhirs** 3.5m and 5m high (see Detours).

Refreshments & Provisions: Cloître St-Thégonnec (4.6kms on D111 from Gare de Kermeur); Scrignac (3kms, all uphill from Gare de Scrignac).

N.B. This section passes through sparsely populated countryside with no nearby facilities. Through travellers in a hurry would do best to continue to Poullaouen (see p.103)

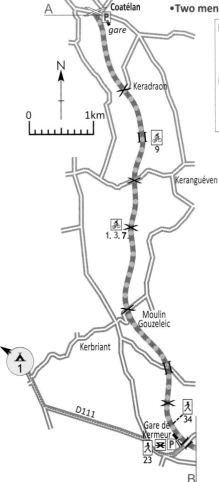

Signage:	▶S - V7 Gare de Scrignac, Poullaouen. ▶N - V7 Coatélan, Morlaix.
Route:	former railway track-bed all the way - easy to follow.
Surface:	compacted sand, fair to good.
Difficulties:	steady climb to Kermeur from either direction.
Detours:	**Wolf Museum** at Cloître St-Thégonnec (⇆10kms). From Gare de Kermeur follow D111 westwards. **Two menhirs** (⇆3kms). From 2nd crossing after bridge at Kermeur, go north, joining D111 right, follow 1.5kms to menhirs on right, before road junction. **Chapel of St-Corentin** (⇆2.5kms). Leave V7 westwards at crossing house 23, then 1st left and continue on track.

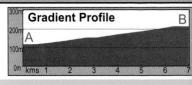

Gradient Profile

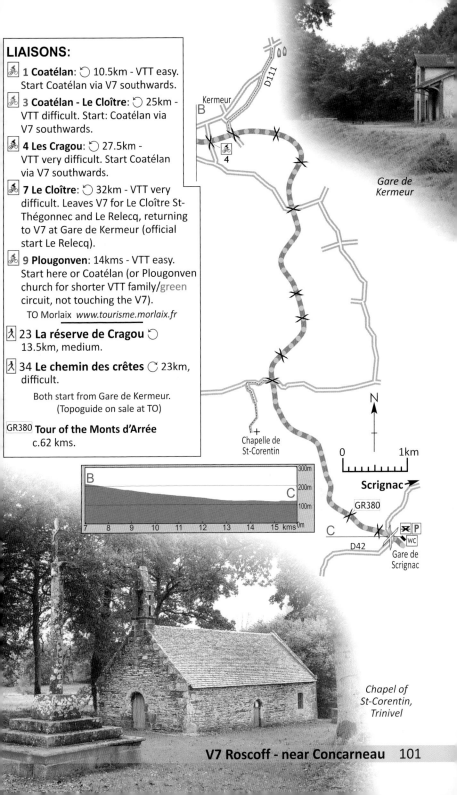

LIAISONS:

🚵 **1 Coatélan**: ↻ 10.5km - VTT easy. Start Coatélan via V7 southwards.

🚵 **3 Coatélan - Le Cloître**: ↻ 25km - VTT difficult. Start: Coatélan via V7 southwards.

🚵 **4 Les Cragou**: ↻ 27.5km - VTT very difficult. Start Coatélan via V7 southwards.

🚵 **7 Le Cloître**: ↻ 32km - VTT very difficult. Leaves V7 for Le Cloître St-Thégonnec and Le Relecq, returning to V7 at Gare de Kermeur (official start Le Relecq).

🚵 **9 Plougonven**: 14kms - VTT easy. Start here or Coatélan (or Plougonven church for shorter VTT family/green circuit, not touching the V7).

   TO Morlaix *www.tourisme.morlaix.fr*

🚶 23 **La réserve de Cragou** ↻ 13.5km, medium.

🚶 34 **Le chemin des crêtes** ↻ 23km, difficult.

   Both start from Gare de Kermeur. (Topoguide on sale at TO)

GR380 **Tour of the Monts d'Arrée** c.62 kms.

Kermeur

D111

B

4

Gare de Kermeur

N

Chapelle de St-Corentin

0   1km

Scrignac

GR380

C

D42

Gare de Scrignac

B   300m / 200m / 100m / 0m   C
7 8 9 10 11 12 13 14 15 kms

Chapel of St-Corentin, Trinivel

The Gare de Scrignac is about half way between Morlaix and Carhaix and, when the railway was operating, served both Scrignac to the north and Berrien to the southwest.

For some distance the V7 has been following the valley of the river Squirriou, but a little short of the road crossing at Kervalon this runs into the Beurc'hoat, which in turn feeds the River Aulne, just before the old stone 3-arched bridge away to the left.

A kilometre after the road crossing here, the river Argent joins the Aulne from the west and on the high ground between the two rivers there is the site of a 11th-12th century motte and bailey. There remain just a few earth banks on the wooded slopes but It's private land so un-explorable. A rather worn-out information panel gives some idea of what it might have looked like.

The old station at Locmaria-Berrien is the centre for hiring horse-drawn caravans (*roulottes* or *calèches*) for an 'alternative' holiday wandering the minor ways of the area.

Continuing over the D769 the Green Way swings eastwards across the Aulne and climbs to Poullaouen.

Signage: ▶S - V7 Poullaouen, Carhaix. ▶N - V7 Gare de Scrignac, Morlaix.
Route: former railway track-bed all the way - easy to follow.
Surface: short stretch of tarmac (good) from Gare de Scrignac, otherwise compacted sand (fair), more stony and uneven south of Locmaria-Berrien.
Difficulties: a few pot-holes. Crossing busy D769, at Locmaria-Berrien and again after Poullaouen.
Detours: Huelgoat (⇆12kms). Take track westwards from crossing just south of bridge over river Argent. Join D769 right and follow 2.5kms, then continue on D769a (D769 goes right to Morlaix).

Places of interest nearby

- **Huelgoat** (detour): Market town (Thurs) with a good range of shops, cafés and restaurants in the market place and opposite the lake.

  Huelgoat is very popular with tourists for its forest and chaos - huge granite rocks tumbled in the valley of the river Argent. The lake is a reservoir for the canal carrying water to power machinery in the now defunct silver mines. Don't miss the Chaos, the '*Gouffre*', Arthurs camp (neolithic/ iron age hill-fort), the Devil's Grotto and the '*Roche Tremblante*' - a large rock that can be moved by applying pressure in exactly the right place.

- **Poullaouen** (pull-ow-en) was important for its silver mine, traces of which can be found at La Mine, just northwest of the *bourg*. In the 18th century the mines at Poullaouen and Locmaria-Berrien were France's principal source of lead and silver. Managers and skilled workers were mostly German with labour recruited locally. The industry declined after rich deposits were discovered in California in 1848.

Roche tremblante, Huelgoat

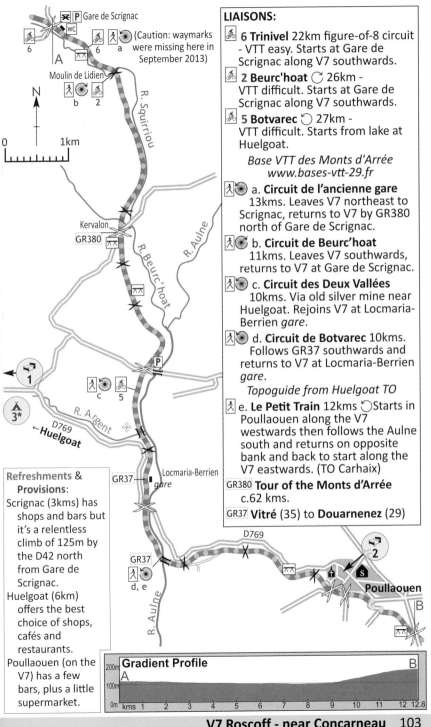

Gare de Scrignac

6   6   a   (Caution: waymarks
                    were missing here in
A   September 2013)

Moulin de Lidien

b   2

N

0   1km

R. Squirriou

Kervalon
GR380

R. Beurc'hoat

R. Aulne

P

c   5

1

3*
←Huelgoat
D769   R. Argent

Refreshments &
Provisions:
Scrignac (3kms) has
shops and bars but
it's a relentless
climb of 125m by
the D42 north
from Gare de
Scrignac.
Huelgoat (6km)
offers the best
choice of shops,
cafés and
restaurants.
Poullaouen (on the
V7) has a few
bars, plus a little
supermarket.

GR37   Locmaria-Berrien
         gare

R. Aulne

GR37
d, e

D769

Poullaouen

B

LIAISONS:

6 Trinivel 22km figure-of-8 circuit
- VTT easy. Starts at Gare de
Scrignac along V7 southwards.

2 Beurc'hoat ↻ 26km -
VTT difficult. Starts at Gare de
Scrignac along V7 southwards.

5 Botvarec ↺ 27km -
VTT difficult. Starts from lake at
Huelgoat.

Base VTT des Monts d'Arrée
www.bases-vtt-29.fr

a. **Circuit de l'ancienne gare**
13kms. Leaves V7 northeast to
Scrignac, returns to V7 by GR380
north of Gare de Scrignac.

b. **Circuit de Beurc'hoat**
11kms. Leaves V7 southwards,
returns to V7 at Gare de Scrignac.

c. **Circuit des Deux Vallées**
10kms. Via old silver mine near
Huelgoat. Rejoins V7 at Locmaria-
Berrien *gare*.

d. **Circuit de Botvarec** 10kms.
Follows GR37 southwards and
returns to V7 at Locmaria-Berrien
gare.

Topoguide from Huelgoat TO

e. **Le Petit Train** 12kms ↺Starts in
Poullaouen along the V7
westwards then follows the Aulne
south and returns on opposite
bank and back to start along the
V7 eastwards. (TO Carhaix)

GR380 **Tour of the Monts d'Arrée**
c.62 kms.

GR37 **Vitré** (35) to **Douarnenez** (29)

Gradient Profile

200m
A   B
100m
0m kms 1   2   3   4   5   6   7   8   9   10 11 12 12.8

For most of the way, this is a quiet section, away from the noise of traffic, through woods and farmland with just the occasional crossing. Even the approach to Carhaix is on a dedicated cycle route, initially alongside the busy main road but soon diverting off to enter Carhaix at a roundabout, between a small and a large supermarket. This is also the point where the V6 leaves the V7.

Carhaix, or Carhaix-Plouguer to give it its full name, lies at the mid-point of western Brittany, now the juncture of three modern *départements*, Finistère, Côtes d'Armor and Morbihan but Carhaix has been a centre of communications since at least Roman times. Its Roman name was *Vorgium* and an extensive area of the Roman town was recently excavated. A 3rd century subterranean aqueduct 27kms long brought water from Maël-Carhaix; the Tourist Office can provide an 'aqueduct trail' to help you find its remnants.

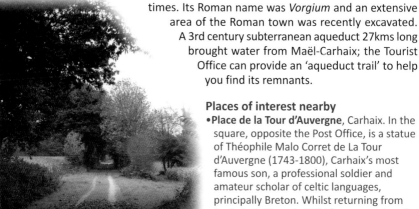

Signage: ▶S - V7 Carhaix, Port de Carhaix.
▶N - V7 Poullaouen, Morlaix.

Surface: compacted sand, fair/poor. In Carhaix, tarmac, variable poor/good.

Difficulties: barriers; narrow path at Le Frostel; town and bypass traffic in Carhaix.

Route: former railway track-bed, then signed route by cycle paths, cycle lanes and roads into and through Carhaix to the car park of 'Éspace Glenmor'.

Detour: Pont Gaulois and Chapelle Ste-Catherine. From Garz an Hore follow road left, over hill to chapel and old stone bridge on right; continue over bridge, up to main road, ahead to parking and re-join V7 route into Carhaix.

Places of interest nearby
- **Place de la Tour d'Auvergne**, Carhaix. In the square, opposite the Post Office, is a statue of Théophile Malo Corret de La Tour d'Auvergne (1743-1800), Carhaix's most famous son, a professional soldier and amateur scholar of celtic languages, principally Breton. Whilst returning from Spain to Brittany in 1794 he was captured when his ship was taken by a British privateer off Camaret. While a prisoner in England he wrote a dictionary of Celtic languages. Released in 1797 and back in Paris, he volunteered as a simple grenadier to serve in place of the last remaining grandson of an old friend. He refused all promotion (he had formerly served in the capacity of general although declining to accept the rank) and consequently he became known as '*premier grenadier de la République*'. He was killed in action on 27th June 1800, the eve of the Battle of Oberhausen. Until 1814 his regiment still called his name at roll call, the most senior sergeant answering '*Mort au champ d'honneur*'.
- **Carhaix station**. Near the station (passed on route) is a steam locomotive that used to work the metre gauge Réseau Breton (see p.28). On the other side of the railway (go under the bridge and turn left) is one of the last railcars to work the old routes that the V7 and V6 now follow.

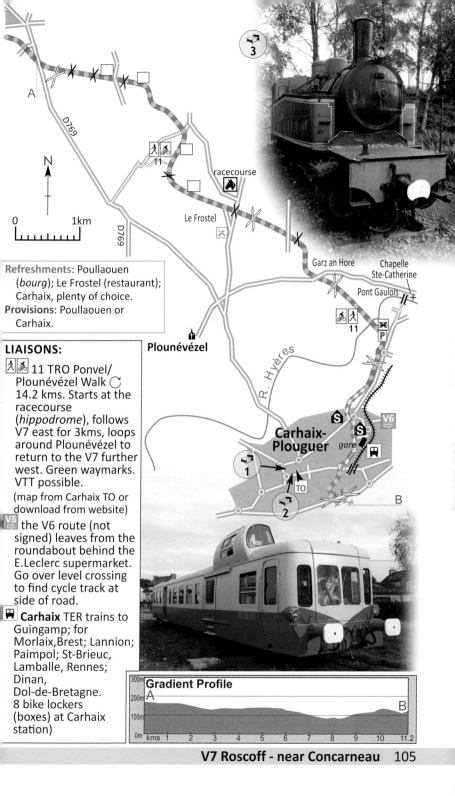

A

N

0   1km

D769

D769

racecourse

Le Frostel

Garz an Hore   Chapelle
Ste-Catherine

Pont Gaulois

11

P

Plounévézel

R. Hyères

Carhaix-
Plouguer   *gare*

TO

B

Refreshments: Poullaouen
(*bourg*); Le Frostel (restaurant);
Carhaix, plenty of choice.
Provisions: Poullaouen or
Carhaix.

LIAISONS:

11 TRO Ponvel/
Plounévézel Walk ↻
14.2 kms. Starts at the
racecourse
(*hippodrome*), follows
V7 east for 3kms, loops
around Plounévézel to
return to the V7 further
west. Green waymarks.
VTT possible.

(map from Carhaix TO or
download from website)

the V6 route (not
signed) leaves from the
roundabout behind the
E.Leclerc supermarket.
Go over level crossing
to find cycle track at
side of road.

Carhaix TER trains to
Guingamp; for
Morlaix,Brest; Lannion;
Paimpol; St-Brieuc,
Lamballe, Rennes;
Dinan,
Dol-de-Bretagne.
8 bike lockers
(boxes) at Carhaix
station)

Gradient Profile

300m
200m
A
100m
0m   kms   1   2   3   4   5   6   7   8   9   10   11.2

B

Following the old railway southwards, the V7 soon reaches Port de Carhaix on the Nantes-Brest Canal, from where a branch went west to Camaret. This has been converted to Green Way as far as Pont Triffen (11kms. See p.70).

The V7 continues south to the northern slopes of the Black Mountains (named after their slate). Motreff was renowned for its slate quarries, sharing this occupation with other communities on the southern side, towards Gourin.

Signage: ▶S - V7 Port de Carhaix; Gourin.
▶N - V7 Carhaix.

Route: former railway track-bed. At the N164 there is a short detour west to join a minor road under the motorway.
At Koad Goaranwareg descend to road, turn left, ignore the bridge, then turn right on concrete path beside house, continue on steep track, hair-pin left over hill to rejoin line of railway on other side.

Surface: compacted sand (fair). In many places it has matured to just a grassy path with two parallel cycle tracks.

Difficulties: bridge removed just south of N164 - steep descent to cross road.
Crossing busy D769 at Port de Carhaix, ▶S turn left 50m then cross to track opposite.
Narrow path and steep hill at Koad Goaranwareg.

Detour: ▶S **St Hernin** (7.5kms) At Port de Carhaix, go through car park and turn left onto D82. After 1km see Calvaire de Kerbreudeur on left. Continue on D82 to St-Hernin. Turn left by church and left again to pass cemetery, continue 2kms to right turn to Chapelle St-Sauveur. Return to road, carry on to T-junction and turn left. *Either* dismount and climb bank to right of bridge to rejoin V7, *or* go under bridge and follow road right, join D769 and turn right under next bridge to rejoin V7 route at Koad Goaranwareg.

LIAISONS:

V6 New section of V6 to Pont Triffen (11kms)

1. **Le Canal de Nantes à Brest** ↻12.4kms. Starts in Carhaix (church of St-Trémeur, near TO). Joins V7 and follows to Pont ar Brost, then canal eastwards, and back to Carhaix. Blue waymarks. VTT possible.

10. **Les Ardoisières** (the slate quarries) ↻16kms. Starts at La Butte du Cheval, goes north to the canal then follows V7 west to Port de Carhaix and south to Moulin Donan, then east and north to return. Yellow waymarks.

14. **L'Argoat** ↻ 17kms. Starts from St-Hernin (*mairie*), joins V7 at Bonne Chance, north to Port de Carhaix then west along canal. Yellow waymarks. VTT possible.

15. **La Montagne** ↻ 12kms, variant 16kms. Circuit on the Black Mountains, returning to the V7 at Pont Kervran. VTT possible.
(map from Carhaix TO or downloads from website)

GR37 **Vitré**(35) to **Douarnenez**(29) - follows V7 or canal from near Carhaix to Port de Carhaix.

GR38 **Douarnenez** (29) to **Redon** (56).

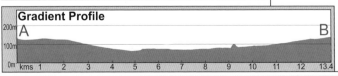

Gradient Profile

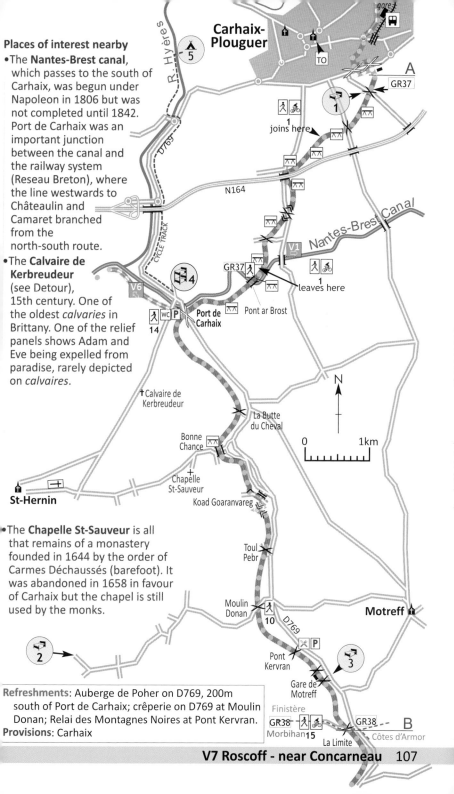

Places of interest nearby

- The **Nantes-Brest canal**, which passes to the south of Carhaix, was begun under Napoleon in 1806 but was not completed until 1842. Port de Carhaix was an important junction between the canal and the railway system (Reseau Breton), where the line westwards to Châteaulin and Camaret branched from the north-south route.

- The **Calvaire de Kerbreudeur** (see Detour), 15th century. One of the oldest *calvaries* in Brittany. One of the relief panels shows Adam and Eve being expelled from paradise, rarely depicted on *calvaires*.

- The **Chapelle St-Sauveur** is all that remains of a monastery founded in 1644 by the order of Carmes Déchaussés (barefoot). It was abandoned in 1658 in favour of Carhaix but the chapel is still used by the monks.

Refreshments: Auberge de Poher on D769, 200m south of Port de Carhaix; crêperie on D769 at Moulin Donan; Relai des Montagnes Noires at Pont Kervran.
Provisions: Carhaix

Carhaix-Plouguer

GR37

N164

Nantes-Brest Canal

1 joins here

1 leaves here

Pont ar Brost

Port de Carhaix

Calvaire de Kerbreudeur

La Butte du Cheval

Bonne Chance

Chapelle St-Sauveur

Koad Goaranvareg

St-Hernin

Toul Pebr

Moulin Donan

Motreff

Pont Kervran

Gare de Motreff

Finistère
Morbihan

GR38

La Limite

Côtes d'Armor

The Black Mountains were exploited in the eighteenth century for their slate deposits but it was at the end of the nineteenth century, with the arrival of the railway you have been riding or walking along, that the industry really flourished. However the quarries had to close in 1962 in the face of stiff competition from the quarries at Trélazé (Angers) and the railway closed soon after.

Gourin has a busy little centre, good for a bite to eat or just to see some people after miles of empty Green Way out of season. In the last week of July the town comes alive with a Pancake Festival - *Fête des Crêpes* - an opportunity to sample the infinite varieties of this Breton gastronomic delight.

Château de Tronjoly

Places of interest nearby
- The 18th century **Château de Tronjoly** is mirrored in the still waters of a former mill-pond, surrounded by a park. It was acquired by the commune in the 1980s and has become a venue for periodic exhibitions and events.

A departmental cycle route (VD1) is a 'project in work' to link Gourin to Le Faouët, Plouay, Pont Scorff and Lorient. At the time of writing it has not reached Gourin, although it is marked prematurely on the official Green Ways map from TOs.

Signage: ▶S - V7 Gourin, Guiscriff, Scaër, Rosporden.
▶N - V7 Gourin, Port de Carhaix, Carhaix.

Route: former railway track-bed most of the way, but interrupted 2kms south of La Limite by major improvements to the D769. Here (▶S) at minor road go left 20m then ahead on track alongside main road, left through tunnel under it, over hill (highest point on this section) to rejoin line of railway for a short way. Through barrier, follow track right, through tunnel, then bear left on either of two parallel tracks and continue on road. At T-junction in Guernéac'h, turn right and left after 50m, back on line of railway. Follow to roundabout and through 2 tunnels to continue alongside road, deviating from it entering Gourin. Continue past the Eco Marché supermarket and cross road to Tourist Office in former railway building. Continue ahead through car park to barrier to rejoin Green Way. Follow to Kerbiquet.

Surface: compacted sand, fair.

Difficulties: Crossing D27 on a blind double bend, south of Gourin.

Detours: Château de Tronjoly (⇆2kms). From Gourin TO, follow GR38 north-west (rue de Toull an Chy) to park and 18th century château. Exhibitions and events in season.
Minguionnet-Guiscriff (11kms). From Gare de Kerbiquet (see p.110).

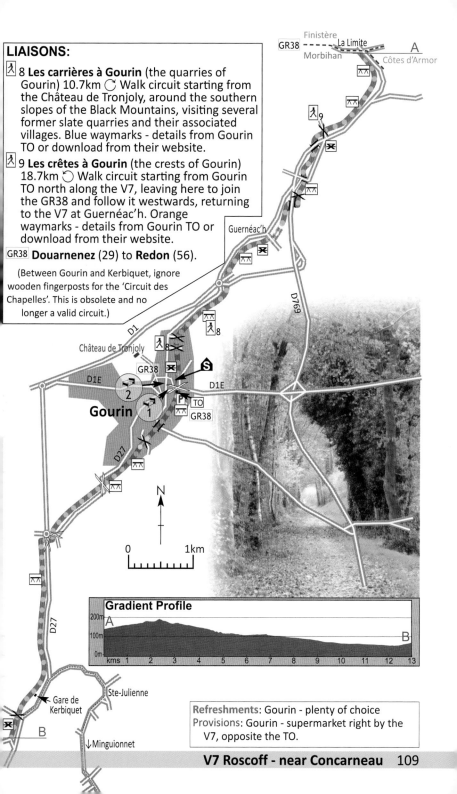

LIAISONS:

8 Les carrières à Gourin (the quarries of Gourin) 10.7km ↻ Walk circuit starting from the Château de Tronjoly, around the southern slopes of the Black Mountains, visiting several former slate quarries and their associated villages. Blue waymarks - details from Gourin TO or download from their website.

9 Les crêtes à Gourin (the crests of Gourin) 18.7km ↺ Walk circuit starting from Gourin TO north along the V7, leaving here to join the GR38 and follow it westwards, returning to the V7 at Guernéac'h. Orange waymarks - details from Gourin TO or download from their website.

GR38 **Douarnenez** (29) to **Redon** (56).

(Between Gourin and Kerbiquet, ignore wooden fingerposts for the 'Circuit des Chapelles'. This is obsolete and no longer a valid circuit.)

Finistère
Morbihan
La Limite
Côtes d'Armor
GR38
A

Guernéac'h

D769

D1

Château de Tronjoly

D1E

Gourin

D1E

D27

N
0 — 1km

D27

Gare de Kerbiquet
Ste-Julienne
↓Minguionnet

B

Gradient Profile

200m
100m
0m
kms 1 2 3 4 5 6 7 8 9 10 11 12 13
A
B

Refreshments: Gourin - plenty of choice
Provisions: Gourin - supermarket right by the V7, opposite the TO.

Still travelling south, this section leaves Morbihan and returns to Finistère at a stream crossing shortly after Guiscriff. At the time of riding this route the change of management was marked by the V7 being meticulously swept by hand in Finistère, while still covered in leaves in Morbihan, but doubtless on a different occasion the roles would be reversed. For a flavour of ultra-deep Breton countryside take the detour via Minguionnet.

Recalling the times when trains rather than cyclists frequented this route, a local association, Association ar Marc'h Du (*marc'h du* = black horse in Breton) has set up a museum at the Gare de Guiscriff, under the name *'Marie monte dans le train'*. It's also an excellent place to stop for refreshments in the museum's café or to stay overnight on their campsite.

From Scaër, the Grande rando 1 (VTT black) presents a challenging alternative route to the south coast via the interesting city of Quimperlé (not to be confused with Quimper). From there, between Clohars-Carnoët and the Bélon estuary, there are several VTT circuits reaching the coast. From Bannalec (on the return leg to Scaër) there is a link to circuit 13 (see p.113, Liaisons) returning to Rosporden, and linking in turn to circuit 12 to Melgven. From here, Concarneau is about 7kms via the D22.

Signage: none on the V7. Circuits are signed but see note under 'Liaisons'.

Route: former railway track-bed all the way - easy to follow.

Surface: compacted sand, fair-good.

Difficulties: two busy road crossings.

Detours: Minguionnet 11kms

▶S ◉ At first road crossing after Halte de Kerbiquet turn left. At T-junction turn left on D27. 750m fork right uphill on minor road. Climb through Le Hellès to Ste-Julienne, bear right passing chapel. Continue past Minguionnet on right. (15th century Minguionnet manor - private). At fork bear right. Half way down hill see Minguionnet alley grave in valley to left. Continue on the road, across another valley and follow through Keryvac'h, Penquernaën and Kervénozaël to T-junction with D187. Turn right and follow to Guiscriff. Turn right (direction Gourin) to find Gare de Guiscriff on left (look for *'Marie monte dans le train'*).

▶N ◐ (as above but in reverse). Leave V7 at Gare de Guiscriff. Turn right on D108, follow 1km to town. Turn left on D187. 600m turn left to Kervénozaël and bear right to Penquernaën. Continue through Keryvac'h and bear left, crossing river valley. Half way up opposite hill see Minguionnet alley grave in valley to right. Continue to top of hill and bear left, passing 15th century Minguionnet manor (private) on left. Continue to Ste-Julienne. Here bear left, down through Le Hellès to join D27, going left. 750m turn right to rejoin V7.

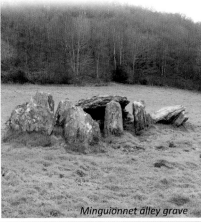
Minguionnet alley grave

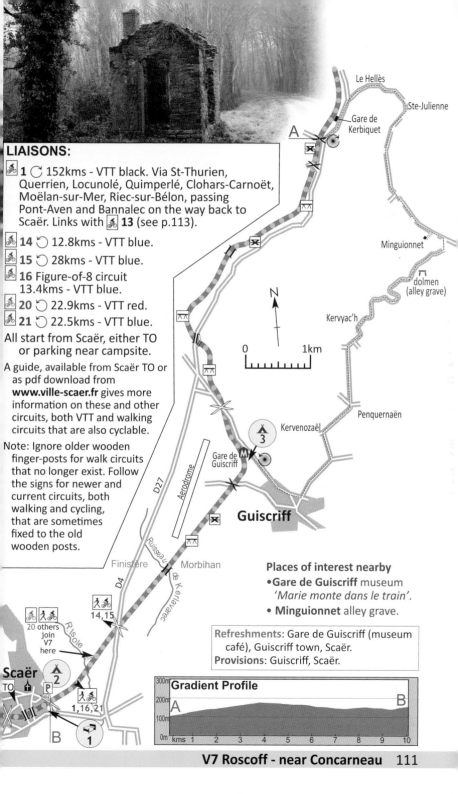

LIAISONS:

🚲 **1** ⟳ 152kms - VTT black. Via St-Thurien, Querrien, Locunolé, Quimperlé, Clohars-Carnoët, Moëlan-sur-Mer, Riec-sur-Bélon, passing Pont-Aven and Bannalec on the way back to Scaër. Links with 🚲 **13** (see p.113).

🚲 **14** ⟳ 12.8kms - VTT blue.

🚲 **15** ⟳ 28kms - VTT blue.

🚲 **16** Figure-of-8 circuit 13.4kms - VTT blue.

🚲 **20** ⟳ 22.9kms - VTT red.

🚲 **21** ⟳ 22.5kms - VTT blue.

All start from Scaër, either TO or parking near campsite.

A guide, available from Scaër TO or as pdf download from **www.ville-scaer.fr** gives more information on these and other circuits, both VTT and walking circuits that are also cyclable.

Note: Ignore older wooden finger-posts for walk circuits that no longer exist. Follow the signs for newer and current circuits, both walking and cycling, that are sometimes fixed to the old wooden posts.

Le Hellès

Ste-Julienne

Gare de Kerbiquet

A

Minguionnet

dolmen (alley grave)

Kervyac'h

N

0   1km

Penquernaën

Kervenozaël

Gare de Guiscriff

Guiscriff

D27

Aerodrome

Ruisseau de Kerlavarec

Finistère   Morbihan

D4

14,15

20 others join V7 here

Risole

Scaër
TO

P

1,16,21

B

1

Places of interest nearby

• **Gare de Guiscriff** museum *'Marie monte dans le train'*.

• **Minguionnet** alley grave.

Refreshments: Gare de Guiscriff (museum café), Guiscriff town, Scaër.
Provisions: Guiscriff, Scaër.

Gradient Profile

300m
A   B
200m
100m
0m kms 1 2 3 4 5 6 7 8 9 10

V7 11. Scaër to Rosporden (12.8kms, Green Way)
TO Scaër 02 98 59 49 37 www.ville-scaer.fr
Rosporden 02 98 59 27 26 www.tourisme-paysderosporden.fr

A few kilometres after Scaër the V7 passes along the northern edge of the Forest of Coatloc'h, where the site of the now demolished Gare de Coatloc'h provides a convenient car park as a base for exploring the forest. According to local tradition the forest was planted in the late Middle Ages under the personal supervision of Anne de Bretagne. It was renowned for its beech trees which provided the raw material for generations of clog-makers.

Signage: none on the V7.

Route: former railway track-bed all the way - easy to follow.

Surface: compacted sand, fair/good.

Detours: Locjean. Leave the V7 at Leign Bigot and take the road southwards, turning right to Locjean. Continue ahead to rejoin the V7.

Refreshments:
Scaër, Rosporden, or bar at Toul ar C'Hoat.
Provisions: Scaër or supermarket 1km west of Scaër. Rosporden.

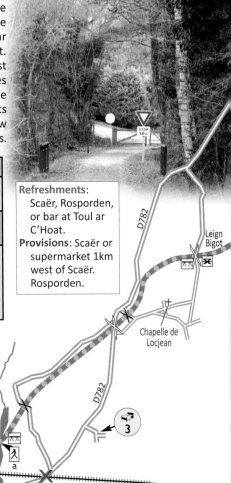

Places of interest nearby

- **Forest of Coatloc'h.** Things to discover include the remnants of a château, and a forester's house (unoccupied since the 1950s). See the Scaër TO website for a map of the forest.
- **Chapelle de Locjean** built by the Hospitalers of St-John of Jerusalem and dating from the 16th century. It has an unusual bell tower, and inside, stone benches line the walls of the nave.
- **Quimper** (24kms west from Rosporden) Cathedral city, capital of Finistère: medieval streets, museums, galleries, restaurants, shopping.

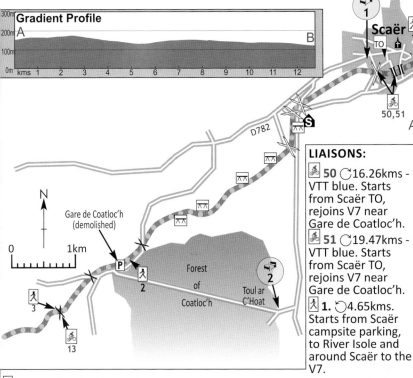

Gradient Profile

300m
200m A   B
100m
0m kms 1   2   3   4   5   6   7   8   9   10   11   12

Scaër

TO

P

50,51

A

LIAISONS:

🚲 **50** ↻16.26kms - VTT blue. Starts from Scaër TO, rejoins V7 near Gare de Coatloc'h.

🚲 **51** ↻19.47kms - VTT blue. Starts from Scaër TO, rejoins V7 near Gare de Coatloc'h.

🚶 **1.** ↻4.65kms. Starts from Scaër campsite parking, to River Isole and around Scaër to the V7.

Gare de Coatloc'h (demolished)

0   1km

N

P

Forest
of
Coatloc'h

Toul ar
C'Hoat

2

2

3

13

D782

🚶 **2. Forest of Coatloc'h** ↻ 8kms. Several variations, starting from the bar at Toul ar C'Hoat and reaching the V7 near the Gare de Coatloc'h.

🚶 **3.** ↻12.26kms (with shortcuts). Via Chapelle de Plascaër, Coadigou and return to V7 at road crossing 350m W of Gare de Coatloc'h.

details of the above from Scaër TO or pdf download from website

🚲 **13** ↻ 31kms - VTT blue. Starts from Rosporden via V7. On its most southerly stretch it is joined by VTT circuit **12**, which can be followed left to Melgven, then it's only 7kms to Concarneau via the D22.

🚶 **a. Histoire et memoires de Rosporden** - cité des étangs (History and memories of Rosporden, city of lakes) ↻ 3.8kms around the lakes.

🚌 **Rosporden** TER trains to Quimper; Vannes. (TER bus only to Concarneau.)

Rosporden, city of lakes.

V7 Roscoff - near Concarneau 113

V7 12. **Rosporden to La Boissière** (8.7kms, signed route)
Rosporden 02 98 59 27 26 www.tourisme-paysderosporden.fr
Concarneau 02 98 97 01 44 www.tourismeconcarneau.fr

The metre gauge Reseau Breton stopped at Rosporden but the V7 continues a little further towards Concarneau. Because the standard gauge branch line from Rosporden to Concarneau is still functional as far as the Triskalia animal feed factory at Coat Conq, the V7 is signed from Rosporden along quieter roads and shady tracks. This signed route passes Coat Conq, ducks under the N165 and terminates, temporarily, at a main road roundabout on the D70 to Concarneau. No doubt eventually the continuation of the branch line, currently neglected and overgrown, will be converted to Green Way as far as Concarneau.

D765
Quimper (23.2kms)

Rosporden

A

gare

D765
Quimperlé
(26kms)

D24
Pont Aven
(15kms)

Locmaria Hent + (chapel)

animal feed factory
Coat Conq

N165

N

D44 B

0   1km

D70
Melgven
D44
Concarneau

Signage:	Concarneau.
Route:	mixed: shared roads & tracks
Surface:	tarmac or compacted sand, good.

Gradient Profile

200m A
100m
0m kms 1   2   3   4   5   6   7   8 8.6
B

WHERE NEXT?

Concarneau, obviously, but within reach to the east are Pont Aven, a pretty river port favoured by Gauguin and other artists, the Belon estuary, famed for oysters, and Quimperlé at the confluence of two rivers, and with some interesting religious monuments as well as the nearby Forêt de Carnoët and Abbaye St Maurice.

To the west lie Fouesnant, Benodet and Pont l'Abbé, from where there is a very pretty Green Way (see p.20) that goes, almost, to Quimper, capital city of Finistère.

*Concarneau
ville close - fortified town*

The V8 is a cycle route across central Brittany from north to south. Only the central portion is on Green Way, where it follows the Rigole d'Hilvern to meet the V6 near St-Caradec and from here share its route westwards to Mûr-de-Bretagne. Just west of Mûr-de-Bretagne the V8 takes the link route (see p.80/1) to join the V1 southwards along the Nantes-Brest Canal to Pontivy. From Pontivy the V8 continues southwards along the Blavet Canal to Hennebont but although perfectly practicable, this stretch of the V8 has not yet been developed as Green Way.

The northern part of the V8 is a recently signed cycle route via minor roads and farm tracks, not a Green Way. It runs for some 40.8kms from Yffiiniac, near St-Brieuc, to Allineuc and the lake at Bosméléac, which is the source of the Rigole d'Hilvern.

*The Rigole d'Hilvern
starts here (on the right)*

The Rigole d'Hilvern and the Barrage de Bosméléac are an extraordinary example of early 19th century engineering. Together they supplied water from the upper reaches of the river Oust to the high point of the Nantes-Brest Canal at Hilvern, where it was needed to replace water lost in the operation of the many locks in both directions along the canal. The Rigole is 63.5kms long, following the contours of the land with a fall of 3cm every 100 metres and was completed in 1838. With the demise of the Nantes-Brest Canal the Rigole fell into disrepair and is now empty for most of its length.

The V8 follows a newly made Green Way running alongside the Rigole. It's a delightfully lazy bike ride with many twists and turns through quiet and hilly countryside.

Places of interest nearby

- **St-Léon** (Merléac) **Chapelle St-Jacques.** Early 14th century chapel noted for its stained glass windows and its wall paintings. It is a stage on the Compostella trail.
- **Uzel**, **L'Atelier-Musée du tissage** A working museum of the local weaving industry and its efforts to meet competition from industrial textiles.
- **Le Quillio** for its church and *enclos paroissal* dating from the 15th century. Other relics of the linen cloth industry include a typical merchant's house and what could now be easily mistaken for a *lavoir* but was originally a linen bleaching tank. The **Site de Lorette** with its *fontaine*, chapel and neolithic *cromlec'h* can be reached by following VTT 9 (see Liaisons)
- **St-Thélo**. Established in a former cloth merchant's house, **La Maison des Toiles** is a museum of the golden age of Breton textiles.

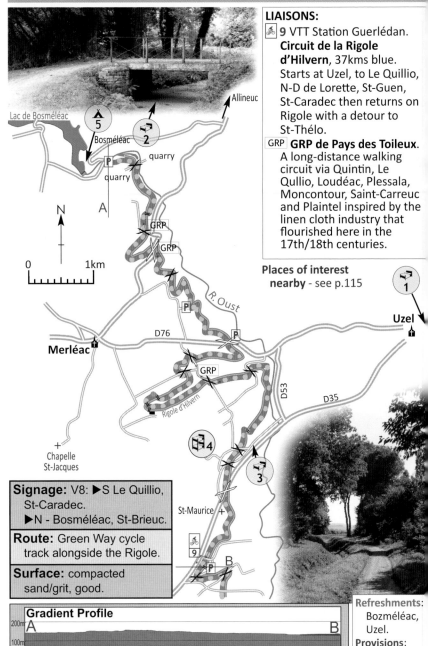

LIAISONS:

🚴 **9** VTT Station Guerlédan. **Circuit de la Rigole d'Hilvern**, 37kms blue. Starts at Uzel, to Le Quillio, N-D de Lorette, St-Guen, St-Caradec then returns on Rigole with a detour to St-Thélo.

GRP **GRP de Pays des Toileux**. A long-distance walking circuit via Quintin, Le Qullio, Loudéac, Plessala, Moncontour, Saint-Carreuc and Plaintel inspired by the linen cloth industry that flourished here in the 17th/18th centuries.

Places of interest nearby - see p.115

Allineuc

Lac de Bosméléac

Bosméléac

quarry

quarry

N

A

0   1km

GRP

GRP

R. Oust

Uzel

D76

Merléac

GRP

Rigole d'Hilvern

D53

D35

Chapelle
St-Jacques

St-Maurice

Signage: V8: ▶S Le Quillio, St-Caradec.
▶N - Bosméléac, St-Brieuc.

Route: Green Way cycle track alongside the Rigole.

Surface: compacted sand/grit, good.

Gradient Profile

200m A
100m
0m kms 1 2 3 4 5 6 7 8 9 10 11 12 13.4
B

Refreshments: Bozméléac, Uzel.
Provisions: Uzel.

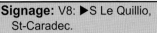

Signage: V8: ▶S Le Quillio, St-Caradec.
▶N - Bosméléac, St-Brieuc.

Route: Green Way cycle track alongside the Rigole.

Surface: compacted sand/grit, good.

LIAISONS:

V6 **V6** Carhaix - St-Méen-le-Grand

9 VTT Station Guerlédan. **Circuit de la Rigole d'Hilvern**.

14 VTT Station Loudéac. **Circuit des Toileux**, 22kms blue. Starts at St-Caradec and follows the Rigole northwards to St-Thélo and returns by road to St-Caradec.

31 Circuit of 12.5kms ↻. Starts from Le Quillio *bourg*, going west to the Site de Lorette, then northeast to return by the Rigole. (*Walks in Côtes d'Armor no.31 - Red Dog Books*).

GRP **GRP de Pays des Toileux**.

GR341 **Bréhec** (north coast) to **Riantec** (south coast). Coming from the north it follows the V6 eastwards from St-Guen, leaves it north again to find the Rigole d'Hilvern, then follows that south.

GR341B alternative route **St-Caradec** to **Hémonstoir** via **Loudéac**.

Refreshments: Le Quillio, St-Thélo, St-Caradec.
Provisions: St-Caradec.

Places of interest nearby - see p.115

The surfaced cycle track continues along the Rigole south of the V6 as far as Hémonstoir. Where it ends turn left on the road, then left at the T junction for Hémonstoir *bourg*.

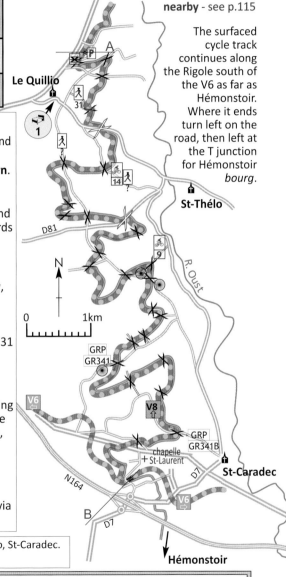

Le Quillio

St-Thélo

D81

N

0   1km

GRP GR341

V6

V8

GRP GR341B

chapelle + St-Laurent

N164

B

D7

V6

Hémonstoir

St-Caradec

R. Oust

Gradient Profile

ACCOMMODATION

This list of accommodation within 5/6kms of the Green Ways has been compiled according to information available in late 2013. It is offered as a guide, without any guarantees as to quality of accommodation or continued availability. Where possible, a website address is given as this is a quick way to confirm availability, price, contact details, etc. One should always make contact in advance before relying on any particular service.

How to use the listings:
On the maps, locate the facilities you want by looking for the appropriate symbol.

Hotel/B&B/   Gîte d'Etape/   camping
Chambre d'hôte   hostel

Note the symbol's number and the page heading to find them in the list.

N.B. The address given for campsites and *gîtes d'étape* is for contact purposes - not necessarily the campsite itself but the person who runs it.

Accueil vélo - cycles welcome
Part of the Green Ways scheme in Brittany is the identification of overnight accommodation of all types - hotels, b&b, gîtes d'étape, camp-sites - that are particularly geared to the needs of cyclists. Bearing the label *'Accueil Vélo'* (cycles welcome) they are situated within 5kms of a cycle route or Green Way and will be able to provide:

• a place to clean your bike, equipped with a tap, hose, brush and sponge
• secure cycle storage
• a repair kit

Other services, either free or charged, usually include:
• tourist information, both general and specific
• clothes and shoe drying facilities
• big breakfasts (continental)
• packed lunches
• evening meal, either on the spot or a restaurant within 1km, or at least the availability of a corner kitchen (except camp-sites - enquire in advance to be sure)
• possibility of an early morning start
• onward transfer of baggage
• details of local cycle repairers
• reservation of cycles for hire

An asterisk* after the number indicates an *'Accueil Vélo'* establishment. Usually, these will also cater specifically for the needs of walkers and horse-riders, though in the latter case it is certainly best to check in advance.

In order to give an adequate and even coverage our list includes many establishments that do not benefit from the *'Accueil vélo'* label. This does not necessarily mean that they are any less aware of the needs of their guests, but if you need to rely on any specific service, such as secure storage for your bike, it is best to enquire in advance.

V2 St-Malo - Rennes

V2/V3 1. St-Malo

Hotels

1* Hôtel Escale Oceania (1.2kms), 76
Chaussée du Sillon, 35400 St-Malo
02 99 40 36 36
escaleoceania.saintmalo@oceaniahotels.com
www.oceaniahotels.com

Gîtes d'étape/hostels

2* Auberge de jeunesse Centre
Patrick Varangot (2kms), 37 avenue
du Révérend-Père Umbricht, 35400
St-Malo 02 99 40 29 80
02 99 40 29 02
info@centrevarangot.com
www.centrevarangot.com

V2/V3 2. Dinard and Pleurtuit

Hotels

1. Hôtel Beaurivage (500m), Place
Général de Gaulle, 35800 Dinard
02 99 46 14 34 (garage for bikes)
www.hotel-beaurivage-dinard.fr

B&B/Chambres d'Hôte

2. M & Mme Bernard (1km), 42 rue de
la Ville des Meniers, 35800 Dinard
02 99 46 27 82
http://clos-d-enhaut.monsite.orange.fr

3. La Ville Patouard (600m), 25 rue de
la Ville Patouard, 22490 Trémereuc
02 96 27 88 29
http://chambrestremereuc.fr

V2/V3 3. Pleslin-Trigavou - Dinan

Hotels

1* Hôtel Les Grandes Tours (1.2km), 6
rue du Château, 22100 Dinan
02 96 85 16 20 carregi@wanadoo.fr
www.lesgrandestours.com

2. Hôtel Arvor (1.5kms), 5 rue Auguste
Pavie, 22100 Dinan 02 96 39 21 22
www.hotelarvordinan.com

B&B/Chambres d'Hôte

3* M & Mme Banks (500m), 5-7 rue
des Grippais, 22100 St-Samson-sur-
Rance 02 96 87 49 70   06 32 59 56 42
reservations@vuedelarance.com
www.vuedelarance.com

Gîtes d'étape/hostels

4* Gîte Beauséjour (2kms), La Hisse,
22100 St-Samson-sur-Rance
02 96 39 53 27   02 96 39 16 05 (mairie)
www.beausejour-camping.com

5* Gîte d'Etape de la Gare (on route),
La Gare, 22490 Pleslin-Trigavou
02 96 27 17 67   06 86 31 26 78
giteetape.pleslintrigavou@orange.fr
www.rando-accueil.com

Camping

6* Camping International La Hallerais
(600m), La Hallerais, 22100 Taden
02 96 39 15 93   02 96 39 94 64
contact@camping-lahallerais.com
www.camping-lahallerais.com

V2 4. Léhon - Evran

Hotels

1* Les 4 Saisons (2.4kms), 5 rue
Guinefort, 22100 Léhon 02 96 39 11 85
www.quatresaisons.eu

B&B/Chambres d'Hôte

2. Chrissie & Dennis Young (200m),
Riverside B&B, 10 rue Anne, Léhon
02 96 87 92 71

3* Domaine Arvor (3kms), La Ville
Ameline, 22100 Tressaint
02 96 39 33 69
contact@domaine-arvor.com
www.chambres-gites-domainearvor.com

4. Les Glycines (600m) 8, Tréliger,
Calorguen 02 96 88 00 08
jc.treliger@wanadoo.fr
http://treliger.free.fr

5. Le Vieux Chien Noir (300m), 1 place
Jean Perrin, 22630 Evran
02 99 27 44 58
www.levieuxchiennoir.com

V2 5. Evran - Tinténiac

Hotels

1* Brit Hotel La Guingette (on route),
1 rue du pont à l'Abesse,
35190 Tinténiac 02 99 68 03 64
contact@hotel-guinguette.com
http://www.hotel-guinguette.com

B&B/Chambres d'Hôte

2. La Clef du Four (3kms), La Touche
Pichard, 35720 Plesder 02 23 22 01 35
06 81 76 40 04   www.laclefdufour.com

3. Le Lézard Tranquille (3kms), 35720
  Pleugueneuc 02 99 69 40 36
  www.lelezardtranquille.fr

Camping

4* Camping Les Peupliers (2kms),
  La Besnelais, 35190 Tinténiac
  02 99 45 49 75
  contact@.domainelespeupliers.fr
  www.domainelespeupliers.fr

V2 6. Hédé - St-Médard

Hotels

1. Hostellerie du Vieux Moulin (2kms),
  La Vallée des Moulins, 35630 Hédé
  02 99 45 45 70
  www.levieuxmoulin-hede.com/

B&B/Chambres d'Hôte

2* Mme Noblaye (100m), La Parfraire,
  35630 Hédé 02 99 45 52 06
  06 73 31 37 17 pnoblaye@neuf.fr
  http://pnoblaye.perso.sfr.fr

3* M & Mme Adgnot (6kms),
  L'Hormondais, 35630 St-Brieuc-des-Iffs
  02 99 45 82 79
  michel.adgnot@wanadoo.fr
  www.hormondais.fr

Camping

4. Camping Aire Naturelle
  Municipale (150m), La Magdeleine,
  35630 Hédé 02 99 45 46 18

5. L'Aire Naturelle Municipale de l'Ille
  (50m), Le Bas Bourg, 35250 St-Médard-
  sur-Ille 02 99 55 23 53

V2 7. St-Germain-sur-Ille - Betton

Hotels

1. Hôtel de la Lévée (250m) 4, avenue
  d'Armorique, 35830 Betton
  02 99 55 81 18
  www.hotelrestaurant-lalevee.fr

B&B/Chambres d'Hôte

2. Chambres d'Hôte Fablet-Roussel
  (3.5kms), La Touche Aubrée, 35830
  Betton 02 99 55 78 56 06 10 03 45 06
  latoucheaubree.free.fr

3. Chambres d'Hôte Besnier (1.3kms),
  Le Bas Chenezé, 35830 Betton
  02 99 55 82 92 06 32 76 58 88

4. Chambres d'Hôte David (1km), La
  Touche Allard, 35520 Melesse
  02 99 66 96 21 06 22 48 95 11
  www.latouche-allard.com

V2 8. St-Gregoire - Rennes

Hotels

1* Hôtel Lecoq Gadby (1.3kms),
  156 rue d'Antrain, 35700 Rennes
  02 99 38 05 55
  contact@lecoq-gadby.com
  www.lecoq-gadby.com

2* Hôtel Mercure Rennes Centre
  (700m), 1 rue Paul Louis Courier, 35000
  Rennes 02 99 78 82 20
  H1056@accor.com
  www.mercure.com

3* Garden Hotel (700m), 3 rue
  Duhamel, 35000 Rennes 02 99 65 45 06
  gardenhotel@wanadoo.fr
  www.hotel-garden.fr

4. Hôtel Anne de Bretagne (700m),
  12 rue Tronjoly, 35000 Rennes
  02 99 31 49 49 www.hotel-rennes.com

5. Hotel des Lices (400m), 7 place des
  Lices, 35000 Rennes 02 99 79 14 81
  hotel.lices@wanadoo.fr
  www.hotel-des-lices.com

Gîtes d'étape/hostels

6* Auberge de Jeunesse (100m), 10-
  12 canal Saint Martin, 35700 Rennes
  02 99 33 22 33 rennes@hifrance.org
  www.fuaj.org/Rennes

V3 Léhon - Questembert
(for St-Malo - Léhon see V2)

V3 4. Léhon - St-André-des-Eaux

Hotels

1* Les 4 Saisons (2.4kms), 5 rue
  Guinefort, 22100 Léhon 02 96 39 11 85
  www.lesquatresaisons.fr.st

B&B/Chambres d'Hôte

2. Chrissie & Dennis Young (200m),
  Riverside B&B, 10 rue Anne, Léhon
  02 96 87 92 71

3* Domaine Arvor (3kms), La Ville
  Ameline, 22100 Tressaint
  02 96 39 33 69
  contact@domaine-arvor.com
  www.chambres-gites-
  domainearvor.com

4* M & Mme Emmett (1km),
  La Priquetais, 22100 Trévron
  02 96 83 56 89 priquetais@orange.fr
  www.lapriquetais.com

V3 5. Le Quiou - Plouasne

B&B/Chambres d'Hôte

1* M & Mme Bernard Huet (2kms),
Callouet, 22830 Plouasne
02 96 86 46 51 www.clevacances.com

V3 6. Médréac - St-Léry

Hotels

1. Hotel l'Adresse (1.3kms), Espace Bel Air
St-Onen-la-Chapelle, 35290 Saint-Méen-
le-Grand 02 23 43 26 00
http://ladresse.brithotel.fr

2. Les 3 Piliers (1km), 5 Place de la
Mairie, 35290 St-Méen-le-Grand
02 99 09 61 68

B&B/Chambres d'Hôte

3* M & Mme de Dieuleveult (300m),
Le Bois Basset, 35290 St-Onen-la-
Chapelle 02 99 09 40 14
http://boisbasset.bcld.net

4.La Ville Février (1.8kms),
56430 Mauron 02 97 22 98 47

Camping

5 La Porte Juhel (300m), 35290
St-Méen-le-Grand 02 99 09 58 04

V3 7. Mauron - Néant-sur-Yvel

Hotels

1* Le Brambily (1km), 14 Place Henri
Thébault, 56430 Mauron
02 97 22 61 67
www.hotel-lebrambily.com

2. Auberge de la Table Rond (2kms), 7
Place de l'Église, 56430 Néant-sur-Yvel
02 97 93 03 96
tableronde56@orange.fr

B&B/Chambres d'Hôte

3. Les Nefliers (600m), La Ville-es-
Mélais, 56430 Mauron (also groups)
02 97 22 90 42 www.les-nefliers.com

Gîtes d'étape/hostels

4* Le Val sans Retour (5kms), 5 rue de
Brocéliande, 56430 Tréhorenteuc
02 97 93 08 08 http://rando.abri.free.fr

Camping

5. Aire de Camping de St-Léry
(2.3kms), 56430 St-Léry 02 97 22 68 76

V3 8. Loyat - Ploërmel

Hotels

1. Hôtel Le Cobh (800m), 10 rue des
Forges, 56800 Ploërmel 02 97 74 00 49
www.hotel-lecobh.com

2. Le Thalassa (150m), 76 rue de la
Gare, 56800 Ploërmel 02 97 72 07 65

B&B/Chambres d'Hôte

3* M & Mme Ardouin-Lachaume
(300m) Château de Saint Malo,
56800 Ploërmel 02 97 73 58 20
www.chateau-saint-malo.com

Camping

4. Camping Merlin l'Enchanteur
(50M), Vallée de l'Yvel, 56800 Loyat
02 97 93 05 52 Open all year
www.campingmerlin.com

V3 9. Montertelot - Malestroit

Hotels

1. Hôtel Le Cap Horn (1.5kms),
1 faubourg Saint-Michel, 56140
Malestroit 02 97 75 13 01
www.hotel-malestroit.com

2* Le Petit Keriquel (1.2kms), 1 Place
de l'église, 56460 La Chapelle-Caro
02 97 74 82 44
lepetitkeriquel@orange.fr
www.keriquel.com

B&B/Chambres d'Hôte

3. La Maison Blanche (1.5Kms from V3
but on canal towpath), 2 rue Madame,
56140 Malestroit 02 97 72 29 09
www.alamaisonblanche.eu

4. Mme Bocandé Le Carouge: 56140
Saint Marcel 02 97 43 12 37
jean.bocande@wanadoo.fr

Gîtes d'étape/hostels

5. L'Écluse (1.6kms), 56140 Malestroit
02 97 75 11 75

Camping

6. Domaine du Roc (750m from V3 but
on canal towpath), Rue Beaurivage,
56460 Le Roc St-André 02 97 74 91 07
www.domaine-du-roc.com

V3 10. Malestroit - Molac

Hotels

1. Manoir de la Combe (1.5kms), La
Combe d'en Haut, 56140 Pleucadeuc
02 97 49 99 50
www.manoir-de-la-combe.com

B&B/Chambres d'Hôte

2. **Thibault** (850m) 20 rue du Général de Gaulle, 56140 St-Marcel 02 97 75 17 42

3 **Moulin de la Beraudaie** (3kms) 56140 Bohal 02 97 73 78 92 06 60 61 14 82 thiclo2@wanadoo.fr

Camping

4. **Camping municipal de la Daufresne** (1.6kms), Chemin des Tanneurs, 56140 Malestroit May- mid Sept 02 97 75 13 33

V3 11. Questembert

Hotels

1 **Le Relais de Bel Air** (on route), 1 ave. Bocquenay, 56230 Questembert 02 97 26 17 61 lerelaisdebelair@orange.fr

2 **Hôtel-Restaurant le Sainte-Anne** (on route), 19 avenue de la Gare), 56230 Questembert 02 97 26 11 47 lesaintanne@wanadoo.fr www.lesaintanne-questembert.fr

B&B/Chambres d'Hôte

3 **Mme Marie-Thérèse Elain** (3kms), Le Haut Mounouff, 56230 Questembert 02 97 26 60 72 bernard.elain@wanadoo.fr

Camping

4 **Camping Municipal de Célac** (1km), Célac, 56230 Questembert 02 97 26 11 24 (in season), 02 97 26 11 38 (out of season) accueil@mairie-questembert.fr

---

V6 Carhaix - St-Méen-Le-Grand

V6 0. Carhaix - Maël-Carhaix

B&B/Chambres d'Hôte

1. **Ferme équestre La Haie Du** (1km) La Haie Du, 29270 Saint-Hernin 02 98 81 74 41 06 08 43 30 91

2. **Annie Et Jacques Le Borgne** (4.5km) Kerhervé, 29270 Cléden-Poher 02 98 93 61 18   06 71 28 73 56 annieleborgne29@aol.com

---

V6 1. Carhaix - Maël-Carhaix

B&B/Chambres d'Hôte

1. **M & Mme Coomber** (400m), La Croix Neuve, 22340 Le Moustoir 02 98 93 08 37 coomber@orange.fr www.holidayinbrittany.org

Camping

2. **Aire Naturelle de l'Étang des Sources** (1km), Kervougard, 22340 Maël-Carhaix 02 96 24 64 12

V6 2. Maël-Carhaix- Plouguernevel

Hotels

1* **Hôtel Henri IV** (250m) Kerbanel, 22110 Rostrenen 02 96 29 15 17 02 96 29 26 67 henri4-medicis@wanadoo.fr www.henri4-medicis.com

B&B/Chambres d'Hôtes

2. **Boconnec** (4km), 22110 Plouguernével 02 96 29 14 09 mobile: 06 67 35 46 05 boconnec@orange.fr www.bokoneg.com

3. **Chambres d'hôtes Burlot** (2kms), 10 rue de la Corderie, 22110 Rostrenen 02 96 29 09 75

Gîtes d'étape/hostels

4* **Gîte d'étape de Kermarc'h** (3kms), Kermarc'h, 22110 Plouguernével 02 96 29 10 95 06 73 55 60 31 02 96 36 04 56 village.kermarc@orange.fr www.plouguernevel.com/kermarch

Camping

5* **Village Vacances de Kermarc'h** (3kms), Kermarc'h, 22110 Plouguernével 02 96 29 10 95 06 73 55 60 31 02 96 36 04 56 village.kermarc@orange.fr www.plouguernevel.com/kermarch

---

V6 3. Plouguernével - St-Gelven

Hotels

1. **Les Jardins de l'Abbaye hotel** (100m), Bon Repos, 22570 St-Gelven 02 96 24 95 77 jardinsabbaye@yahoo.fr www.jardinsabbaye.fr

B&B/Chambres d'Hôte

2. **Linda West** (500m), Ty Aven, 45 Rue du Moulin, 22570 Gouarec 02 96 24 87 99 www.tyaven.com trevnlinda@orange.fr trevnlinda@aol.co.uk

Gîtes d'étape/hostels

3* **Gîte d'étape de la Gare** (40m), 22570 Gouarec 06 77 38 05 95

4* **Gîte d'étape de Laniscat** (4kms),15 rue de Pen Ar Choad, 22570 Laniscat 06 87 43 65 69 www.laniscat.fr

Camping

5. **Camping Tost Aven**(400m), Le Bout du Pont, 22570 Gouarec (May- mid Sept) 02 96 24 87 86   06 03 35 19 65 bertrand.cocherel@orange.fr campingdegouarec.free.fr

V6 4. St-Gelven - St-Guen

Hotels

1. **Le Beau Rivage Hôtel** (2kms), Caurel (500m), Beau Rivage, 22530 Caurel 02 96 28 52 15 lebeaurivage22@orange.fr

2* **Le Relais du Lac** (200m), Rue Roc'hell, 22530 Caurel 02 96 67 11 00 / 02 96 67 11 09 relaisdulaccaurel@wanadoo.fr www.hotel-restaurant-bretagne.fr

3. **La Vallée** (5kms), Le Bourg, 22530 St-Gilles-Vieux-Marché 02 96 28 53 32

4.**La Perrière** (500m), 2 rue des Ardoisiers, 22530 Mur-de-Bretagne 02 96 26 08 63

B&B/Chambres d'Hôte

5* **Le Boudec Odile** (4kms), Le Pont Guern, 22530 Mûr de Bretagne 02 96 28 54 52 leboudec.yannick@neuf.fr www.tycanal.com

6. **Mme Le Bozec** (200m) 3 Kergoff, route du lac, Caurel 02 96 28 59 47 06 82 18 54 63 ma.lebozec@orange.fr

7. **M & Mme Partridge** (400m) Pearblossom House, rue de la Résistance, 22530 Mûr de Bretagne 02 96 26 07 89 · contact@pearblossomhouse.com www.pearblossomhouse.com

Gîtes d'étape/hostels

8* **Gîte d'étape de Caurel** (500m), Le Bourg, 22530 Caurel 02 96 28 52 21 mairie-caurel@orange.fr

9. **(groups only) Base Plein Air de Guerlédan** (1km), 106 rue du Lac, 22530 Mur-de-Bretagne 02 96 67 12 22 www.base-plein-air-guerledan.com

10* **Gîte d'étape de St-Guen** (500m), Place du Sénéchal, 22530 Saint-Guen 06 80 73 22 25

Camping

11* **Camping Nautic International** (1km), Beau Rivage, 22530 Caurel 02 96 28 57 94 campingnautic.free.fr

12* **Camping Le Point de Vue** (2kms), 104 rue du Lac, 22530 Mur-de-Bretagne 02 96 26 01 90 06 80 25 87 21 camping-lepointdevue@orange.fr www.camping-lepointdevue.fr

V6 5. St-Guen - Loudéac

Hotels

1. **Les Routiers** (1km), 7 Rue Lavergne, BP 616, 22600 Loudéac 02 96 28 01 44

2* **Hotel Le France** (1km), Place de l'Église, 22600 Loudéac 02 96 66 00 15 lefrance@hotel-loudeac.com www.hotel-loudeac.com

3* **Hotel Voyageurs** (1km), Monsieur Eric Gautier, 10 rue de Cadelac, 22600 Loudéac 02 96 28 00 47 / 02 96 28 22 30 hoteldesvoyageurs@wanadoo.fr www.hoteldesvoyageurs.fr

B&B/Chambres d'Hôte

4* **Mme Marie Chauvel** (3kms), La Ville aux Veneurs, 22600 Trévé 02 96 25 02 02   06 82 94 96 35

5* **M & Mme Caille** (8oom), 11 Place du champ de Foire, 22600 St-Caradec 02 96 25 17 55 laprevenchere@wanadoo.fr www.beautifulbrittany.com

6* **M & Mme Le Maître** (1km), Goizel, 22600 Saint-Caradec 02 96 25 05 30 / 06 20 15 68 12 loiclemaitre@wanadoo.fr www.gitesdarmor.com/goizel

7* Mme Donnio-Nagat (800m),
La Theilo, 22600 Saint-Caradec
02 96 25 02 66 / 06 80 20 34 11
githilvern@wanadoo.fr
www.gitesdarmor.com/lhilvern

V6 6. Loudéac - Plémet

Hotels

1* Hostellerie du Mené (3kms), 2 rue
des Fraîches, 22210 Plémet
02 96 25 61 54 hoteldumene@aol.fr

Gîtes d'étape/hostels

2* Pont Querra (on route), 22210
Plémet 02 96 28 25 17   02 96 26 84 98

Camping

3. Camping Municipal des Ponts-Es-
Bigots (1.5km), Ponts-Es-Bigots, 22600
Loudéac 02 96 66 85 00
www.aquarev-loudeac.fr

4. Camping Municipal des Noës
(1km), Les Noës, 22210 La Prénessaye
02 96 25 64 81   02 96 25 64 81

5. Camping municipal du Pré de la
Mare (3kms), La Croix Nouette, 22210
Plémet 02 96 25 61 10

V6 7. Laurenan - Merdrignac

B&B/Chambres d'Hôte

1* M & Mme Guillory (4kms),
Roquetton, 22230 Gomené
02 96 67 49 08 / 06 74 59 05 96

Camping

2* Camping Val de Landrouët
(on route), Le Val, 22230 Merdrignac
02 96 28 47 98
camping.merdrignac@orange.fr
www.valdelandrouet.com

V6 9. St-Méen-Le-Grand

Hotels

1. Hotel l'Adresse (1.3kms), Espace Bel
Air, St-Onen-la-Chapelle, 35290 Saint-
Méen-le-Grand 02 23 43 26 00
http://ladresse.brithotel.fr

2. Les 3 Piliers (1km), 5 Place de la
Mairie, 35290 St-Méen-le-Grand
02 99 09 61 68

3* M & Mme De Dieuleveult (5kms
but near V3 route), Le Bois Basset,
35290 Saint-Onen-la-Chapelle
02 99 09 40 14
p.a.dedieuleveult@wanadoo.fr
http://boisbasset.bcld.net

Camping

4. Camping La Porte Juhel (3kms),
35290 Saint-Méen-le-Grand
02 99 09 58 04

V7 Roscoff - Concarneau

V7 1. Roscoff - Lanvéguen

Hotels

1* Hôtel Armen Le Triton (2kms),
Rue du Docteur Bagot, 29680 Roscoff
02 98 61 24 44
resa@hotel-letriton.com
www.hotel-letriton.com

2* Hôtel La Résidence (2kms) Rue des
Johnnies 02 98 69 74 85
www.hotelroscoff-laresidence.fr

3* Hôtel du Cheval Blanc (100m) 6 rue
au Lin, 29250 St-Pol-de-Léon
02 98 69 01 00
contact@hotelchevalblanc.com
www.hotelchevalblanc.com

4* Hôtel Le Passiflore (700m),
28 rue Pen ar Pont, 29250 St-Pol-de-
Léon 02 98 69 00 52
contact@hotel-restaurant-lepassiflore.fr
www.hotel-restaurant-lepassiflore.fr

Camping

5* Camping Aux Quatre Saisons
(3.5kms), Perharidy, Le Ruguel, 29680
Roscoff. Apr-Oct   02 98 69 70 86
campingaux4saisons@wanadoo.fr
www.camping-aux4saisons.com

6* Camping Ar Kleguer (1.5km), Plage
Ste-Anne, 29250 St-Pol-de-Léon.
Apr-Sept 02 98 69 18 81
info@camping-ar-kleguer.com
www.camping-ar-kleguer.com

V7 3. Morlaix

Hotels

1 Hôtel de la Gare (450m) 25 Place
St-Martin, 29600 Morlaix
02 98 88 03 29

2 Hôtel du Port (50m) 3 Quai Léon,
29600 Morlaix 02 98 88 07 54
info@lhotelduport.com
www.lhotelduport.com

3. Hôtel-Restaurant Saint-Melaine
(300m) 75-77 rue Ange de Guernisac,
29600 Morlaix 02 98 88 54 76
www.hotel-saint-melaine.com

B&B/Chambres d'Hôte

4* Manoir de Coat Amour (on route)
M & Mme Taylor, Route de Paris, 29600
Morlaix. 02 98 88 57 02
stafford.taylor@wanadoo.fr
www.gites-morlaix.com

5. Ty Pierre (on route) 1bis Place de
Viarmes, 29600 Morlaix.
Pierre-Yves Jacquet   02 98 63 25 75/
06 80 01 37 75
pierreyvesjacquet@hotmail.com
http://lenaj.free.fr/typierre/

Gîtes d'étape/hostels

6. Auberge de Jeunesse (500m), 1 Voie
d'Accès au Port, 29600 Morlaix
02 98 15 10 55
morlaix@aj-finistere.org
www.aj-morlaix.org

V7 4. Morlaix - Coatélan

Hotels

1* Cozy Hotel (3kms), Prat Alan, Route
Départementale 712,
29610 Plouigneau. Tel 02 98 88 08 68,
http://www.cozyhotel-morlaix.com

B&B/Chambres d'Hôte

2* Mme Hélary (5km), Lestrézec, 29600
Plourin-les-Morlaix. 02 98 72 53 55
phelary@yahoo.fr
http://pagesperso-orange.fr/tourisme.bretagne

V7 5. Coatélan - Scrignac

Camping

1 Camping des Bruyères (5kms), 29410
Le Cloître St-Thégonnec 02 98 79 71 76
judi.peate@yahoo.com

V7 6. Scrignac - Poullaouen

B&B/Chambres d'Hôte

1 Les Glycines (6km), 7 rue du docteur
Jacq, 29690 Huelgoat 02 98 99 90 26
paolo.santoro@orange.fr
www.lesglycinesbandb.com

2. Auberge de la Tour d'Auvergne
(300m), 29246 Poullaouen
02 98 93 52 64
www.auberge-delatourdauvergne.com

Camping

3* Camping La Rivière d'Argent
(3kms), M. Berthelot, La Coudraie,
29690 Huelgoat 02 98 99 72 50
campriviere@wanadoo.fr
www.lariviEredargent.com

V7 7. Poullaouen - Carhaix

Hotels

1. Noz Vad (1km), 12 Blvd. de la
République, 29270 Carhaix-Plouguer
02 98 99 12 12 aemcs@nozvad.com
www.nozvad.com

2. Bar Hôtel d'Ahès (1km)1,3 rue
Ferdinand Lancien, 29270 Carhaix
02.98.93.00.09 www.hotel-ahes.com

B&B/Chambres d'Hôte

3. Julia Brailsford (2.5km) Kermoine,
29270 Plounévézel 02 98 99 19 64
julia@lekoru.com www.lekoru.com

V7 8. Carhaix - La Limite

B&B/Chambres d'Hôte

1. Peter & Penny Dinwiddie (on
route), Manoir de Kerlédan, 29270
Carhaix-Plouguer 02 98 99 44 63
info@kerledan.com
www.kerledan.com

2. Domaine de Koadig (3km), Coadic,
29270 St-Hernin (B&B and gîte d'étape)
02 98 99 50 57 dd.leal@wanadoo.fr
www.ddleal.com

3. Le Ruisseau (200m), La Gare de
Motreff, 29270 Motreff 02 98 81 74 08
booking@leruisseau.info
www.leruisseau.info

4. Gite d'étape de Port de Carhaix
(200m) 29270 Carhaix-Plouguer
02 98 99 58 84   06 07 10 03 24
06 11 82 05 79
portdecarhaix@gmail.com
www.portdecarhaix.fr

Camping

5. Camping Municipal de la Vallée de
l'Hyères (3.5km), 29270 Carhaix
02 98 99 10 58
valleedelhyeres@wanadoo.fr

V7 9. La Limite - Kerbiquet

Hotels

1. La Chaumière (200m), 3 Rue de la
Libération, 56110 Gourin
02 97 23 43 02

B&B/Chambres d'Hôte

2. Joëlle Libé (400m) 15 rue de Carhaix
56110 Gourin 02 97 23 58 36
joelle.libe@orange.fr

V7 10. Kerbiquet - Scaër

B&B/Chambres d'Hôte

1. Les Trois Fontaines (500m), Gayna or John Campbell, 15 Rue Desiré Granet, 29390 Scaër. 02 98 57 63 03
info@.jc-lestroisfontaines.com
www.jc-lestroisfontaines.com

Camping

2. Camping Municipal de Kerisole (400m), Rue Louis Pasteur, 29390 Scaër 02 98 57 60 91 / 06 86 00 11 74 (mid June- end Aug) 02 98 59 42 10 (out of season) www.ville-scaer.fr

3. Camping de la Gare de Guiscriff (on route), Association Ar Marc'h Du, 117 rue de la Gare, 56560 Guiscriff. (April- Sept) 02 97 34 15 80
armarchdu.guiscriff@orange.fr
www.lagaredeguiscriff.com

V7 11. Scaër - Rosporden

B&B/Chambres d'Hôte

1. Pierrette Capitaine (300m) 5 rue Laënnec, 29390 Scaër 02 98 59 42 16
www.le-clos-st-andre.com

2. Le Toul ar C'Hoat (2.5km), Forêt de Coat loch, 29390 Scaër. 02 98 59 00 77
contact@etape-bretagne.com
www.etape-bretagne.com

3. Les Pieds dans l'Herbe (2km), Kerantou, 29140 Rosporden
06 64 25 43 22
www.lespiedsdanslherbe-bretagne.com

V7 12. Rosporden - La Boissière

B&B/Chambres d'Hôte

1. M et Mme Le Brigand (300m) L'orée de l'Océan, La Boissière, 29900 Concarneau 02 98 97 12 47
06 61 24 32 79
joelleetmichel.le-brigand@wanadoo.fr
loreedelocean.webnode.com

V8 Bosméléac - St-Caradec

V8 1. Bosméléac - Le Quillio

Hotels

1. L'Auberge de l'Oust (2.7kms) 10, rue de la Gare, Uzel 02 96 67 37 80
auberge-oust@orange.fr
www.aubergedeloust.fr

B&B/Chambres d'Hôte

2. Mme Hervo (3kms) Le Guerny, Allineuc 02 96 28 82 34 06 17 33 45 61
gabrielle.hervo@orange.fr

3. M. Cadoret (150m) Domaine de Bizoin, Merléac 02 96 28 81 24
bizoin22@aol.com
www.armoriquebanb.com

Gîtes d'Étape

4. La Perrière (700m) Domaine de la Perrière, Le Quillio (mid April to mid October) 02 96 56 32 35
domainedelaperriere.monsite-orange.fr

Camping

5. Camping de Bosméléac (500m) Le Petit Bosméléac, 22460 Allineuc. Camping high season only, chalets all year. 02 96 28 87 88 06 61 15 27 90
campingdebosmeleac.jimdo.com

V8 2. Le Quillio - St-Caradec

1. M. Le Pottier (700m) Le Bourg, Le Quillio 02 96 56 38 81
06 86 96 28 96
lepottierdomicile.franck@neuf.fr

(See also V6 5 for St-Caradec, p.123)

Journey Planner

Day	Map section	Accommodation	Contact

Journey Planner

Day	Map section	Accommodation	Contact

Journey Planner

Day	Map section	Accommodation	Contact

Distances in kilometres (corrected to one decimal place)
Shows the distance from point A on any map to point A or B on any other map
(point B on one map will be the same as point A on the following map, therefore point A is used throughout, except for the final point B of a route)

	V2/V3 1A	V2/V3 2A	V2/V3 3A	V2 4A	V2 5A	V2 6A	V2 7A	V2 8A	V2 8B	V3 4A	V3 5A	V3 6A	V3 7A	V3 8A	V3 9A	V3 10A	V3 11A	V3 11B	V6 9B	V6 9A	V6 8A
V8 1A	171	167	157	141.8	137.7	158.8	181.1	195.9	205.5	141.8	123.2	112.6	109.9	124.1	137.1	148.7	160.8	168.9	91.6	86.4	74.8
V8 2A	157.6	153.6	143.6	128.4	124.3	145.4	167.7	182.5	192.1	128.4	109.8	99.2	96.5	110.7	123.7	135.3	147.4	155.5	78.2	73	61.4
V8 2B	141	137	127	111.8	107.7	128.8	151.1	165.9	175.5	111.8	93.2	82.6	79.9	94.1	107.1	118.7	130.8	138.9	61.6	56.4	44.8
V7 1A	284.8	280.8	270.8	255.6	251.5	272.6	294.9	309.7	319.3	254.6	237.1	226.4	223.7	237.9	250.9	262.5	274.6	282.7	205.4	200.2	188.6
V7 2A	272.8	268.8	258.8	243.6	239.5	260.6	282.9	297.7	307.3	243.6	225.1	214.4	211.7	225.9	238.9	250.5	262.6	270.7	193.4	188.2	176.6
V7 3A	256.8	252.8	242.8	227.6	223.5	244.6	266.9	281.7	291.3	227.6	209.1	198.4	195.7	209.9	222.9	234.5	246.6	254.7	177.4	172.2	160.6
V7 4A	254.6	250.6	240.6	225.4	221.3	242.4	264.7	279.5	289.1	225.4	206.9	196.2	193.5	207.7	220.7	232.3	244.4	252.5	175.2	170	158.4
V7 5A	246.3	242.3	232.3	217.1	213	234.1	256.4	271.2	280.8	217.1	198.6	187.9	185.2	199.4	212.4	224	236.1	244.2	166.9	161.7	150.1
V7 6A	230.4	226.4	216.4	201.2	197.1	218.2	240.5	255.3	264.9	201.2	182.7	172	169.3	183.5	196.5	208.1	220.2	228.3	151	145.8	134.2
V7 7A	217.6	213.6	203.6	188.4	184.3	205.4	227.7	242.5	252.1	188.4	169.9	159.2	156.5	170.7	183.7	195.3	207.4	215.5	138.2	133	121.4
V7 8A	209.9	205.9	195.9	180.7	176.6	197.7	220	234.8	244.4	180.7	162.2	151.5	148.8	163	176	187.6	199.7	207.8	130.5	125.3	113.7
V7 9A	223.3	219.3	209.3	194.1	190	211.1	233.4	248.2	257.8	194.1	175.6	164.9	162.2	176.4	189.4	201	213.1	221.2	143.9	138.7	127.1
V7 10A	236.3	232.3	222.3	207.1	203	224.1	246.4	261.2	270.8	207.1	188.6	177.9	175.2	189.4	202.4	214	226.1	234.2	156.9	151.7	140.1
V7 11A	246.3	242.3	232.3	217.1	213	234.1	256.4	271.2	280.8	217.1	198.6	187.9	185.2	199.4	212.4	224	236.1	244.2	166.9	161.7	150.1
V7 12A	259.1	255.1	245.1	229.9	225.8	246.9	269.2	284	293.6	229.9	211.4	200.7	198	212.2	225.2	236.8	248.9	257	179.7	174.5	162.9
V7 12B	267.8	263.8	253.8	238.6	234.5	255.6	277.9	292.7	302.3	238.6	220.1	209.4	206.7	220.9	233.9	245.5	257.6	265.7	188.4	183.2	171.6
V6 0A	226.1	222.1	212.1	196.9	192.8	213.9	236.2	251	260.6	196.9	178.3	167.7	165	179.2	192.2	203.8	215.9	224	146.7	141.5	129.9
V6 1A	208.2	204.2	194.2	179	174.9	196	218.3	233.1	242.7	179	160.4	149.8	147.1	161.3	174.3	185.9	198	206.1	128.8	123.6	112
V6 2A	196.3	192.3	182.3	167.1	163	184.1	206.4	221.2	230.8	167.1	148.5	137.9	135.2	149.4	162.4	174	186.1	194.2	116.9	111.7	100.1
V6 3A	181.3	177.3	167.3	152.1	148	169.1	191.4	206.2	215.8	152.1	133.5	122.9	120.2	134.4	147.4	159	171.1	179.2	101.9	96.7	85.1
V6 4A	164.7	160.7	150.7	135.5	131.4	152.5	174.8	189.6	199.2	135.5	116.9	106.3	103.6	117.8	130.8	142.4	154.5	162.6	85.3	80.1	68.5
V6 5A	145.9	141.9	131.9	116.7	112.6	133.7	156	170.8	180.4	116.7	98.1	87.5	84.8	99	112	123.6	135.7	143.8	66.5	61.3	49.7
V6 6A	128.7	124.7	114.7	99.5	95.4	116.5	138.8	153.6	163.2	99.5	80.9	70.3	67.6	81.8	94.8	106.4	118.5	126.6	49.3	44.1	32.5
V6 7A	110.1	106.1	96.1	80.9	76.8	97.9	120.2	135	144.6	80.9	62.3	51.7	49	63.2	76.2	87.8	99.9	108	30.7	25.5	13.9
V6 8A	96.2	92.2	82.2	67	62.9	84	106.3	121.1	130.7	67	48.4	37.8	35.1	49.3	62.3	73.9	86	94.1	16.8	11.6	0
V6 9A	84.6	80.6	70.6	55.4	51.3	72.4	94.7	109.5	119.1	55.4	36.8	26.2	23.5	37.7	50.7	62.3	74.4	82.5	5.2	0	11.6
V6 9B	79.4	75.4	65.4	50.2	46.1	67.2	89.5	104.3	113.9	50.2	31.6	21	18.3	32.5	45.5	57.1	69.2	77.3	0	5.2	16.8
V3 11B	155.7	151.7	141.7	126.5	122.4	143.5	165.8	180.6	190.2	126.5	107.9	97.3	59	44.8	31.8	20.2	8.1	0	77.3	82.5	94.1
V3 11A	147.6	143.6	133.6	118.4	114.3	135.4	157.7	172.5	182.1	118.4	99.8	89.2	50.9	36.7	23.7	12.1	0	8.1	69.2	74.4	86
V3 10A	135.5	131.5	121.5	106.3	102.2	123.3	145.6	160.4	170	106.3	87.7	77.1	38.8	24.6	11.6	0	12.1	20.2	57.1	62.3	73.9
V3 9A	123.9	119.9	109.9	94.7	90.6	111.7	134	148.8	158.4	94.7	76.1	65.5	27.2	13	0	11.6	23.7	31.8	45.5	50.7	62.3
V3 8A	110.9	106.9	96.9	81.7	77.6	98.7	121	135.8	145.4	81.7	63.1	52.5	14.2	0	13	24.6	36.7	44.8	32.5	37.7	49.3
V3 7A	96.7	92.7	82.7	67.5	63.4	84.5	106.8	121.6	131.2	67.5	48.9	38.3	0	14.2	27.2	38.8	50.9	59	18.3	23.5	35.1
V3 6A	58.4	54.4	44.4	29.2	25.1	46.2	68.5	83.3	92.9	29.2	10.6	0	38.3	52.5	65.3	77.1	89.2	97.3	21	26.2	37.8
V3 5A	47.8	43.8	33.8	18.6	14.5	35.6	57.9	72.7	82.3	18.6	0	10.6	48.9	63.1	76.1	87.7	99.8	107.9	31.6	36.8	48.4
V3 4A	29.2	25.2	15.2	0	10.7	31.8	54.1	68.9	78.5	0	18.6	29.2	67.5	81.7	94.7	106.3	118.4	126.5	50.2	55.4	67
V2 8B	107.7	103.7	93.7	78.5	67.8	46.4	24.4	9.6	0	78.5	82.3	92.9	131.2	145.4	158.4	170	182.1	190.2	113.9	119.1	130.7
V2 8A	98.1	94.1	84.1	68.9	58.2	37.1	14.8	0	9.6	68.9	72.7	83.3	121.6	135.8	148.8	160.4	172.5	180.6	104.3	109.5	121.1
V2 7A	83.3	79.3	69.3	54.1	43.4	22.3	0	14.8	24.4	54.1	57.9	68.5	106.8	121	134	145.6	157.7	165.8	89.5	94.7	106.3
V2 6A	61	57	47	31.8	21.1	0	22.3	37.1	46.7	31.8	35.6	46.2	84.5	98.7	111.7	123.3	135.4	143.5	67.2	72.4	84
V2 5A	39.9	35.9	25.9	10.7	0	21.1	43.4	58.2	67.8	10.7	14.5	25.1	63.4	77.6	90.6	102.2	114.3	122.4	46.1	51.3	62.9
V2 4A	29.2	25.2	15.2	0	10.7	31.8	54.1	68.9	78.5	0	18.6	29.2	67.5	81.7	94.7	106.3	118.4	126.5	50.2	55.4	67
V2/V3 3A	14	10	0	15.2	25.9	47	69.3	84.1	93.7	15.2	33.8	44.4	82.7	96.9	109.9	121.5	133.6	141.7	65.4	70.6	82.2
V2/V3 2A	4	0	10	25.2	35.9	57	79.3	94.1	103.7	25.2	43.8	54.4	92.7	106.9	119.9	131.5	143.6	151.7	75.4	80.6	92.2
V2/V3 1A	0	4	14	29.2	39.9	61	83.3	98.1	107.7	29.2	47.8	58.4	96.7	110.9	123.9	135.5	147.6	155.7	79.4	84.6	96.2

Note: Distances are based on the GPS trace of the actual route. They can differ from distances shown on signs or published elsewhere, as these may have been measured by other means using different starting points.

V6 7A	V6 6A	V6 5A	V6 4A	V6 3A	V6 2A	V6 1A	V6 0A	V7 12B	V7 12A	V7 11A	V7 10A	V7 9A	V7 8A	V7 7A	V7 6A	V7 5A	V7 4A	V7 3A	V7 2A	V7 1A	V8 2B	V8 2A	V8 1A
60.9	42.3	34.9	53.7	70.3	85.3	97.2	115.1	156.8	148.1	135.3	125.3	112.3	98.9	106.6	119.4	135.3	143.6	145.8	161.8	173.8	30	13.4	0
47.5	28.9	21.5	40.3	56.9	71.9	83.8	101.7	143.4	134.7	121.9	111.9	98.9	85.5	93.2	106	121.9	130.2	132.4	148.4	160.4	16.6	0	13.4
30.9	12.3	4.9	23.7	40.3	55.3	67.2	85.1	126.8	118.1	105.3	95.3	82.3	68.9	76.6	89.4	105.3	113.6	115.7	131.7	143.7	0	16.6	30
174.7	156.1	138.9	120.2	103.6	88.6	76.7	94.5	136.3	127.6	114.8	104.8	91.8	78.4	67.2	54.4	38.5	30.2	28	12	0	143.7	160.4	173.8
162.7	144.1	126.9	108.2	91.6	76.6	64.7	82.5	124.3	115.6	102.8	92.8	79.8	66.4	55.2	42.4	26.5	18.2	16	0	12	131.7	148.4	161.8
146.7	128.1	110.9	92.2	75.6	60.6	48.7	66.5	108.3	99.6	86.8	76.8	63.8	50.4	39.2	26.4	10.5	2.2	0	16	28	115.7	132.4	145.8
144.5	125.9	108.7	90	73.4	58.4	46.5	64.3	106.1	97.4	84.6	74.6	61.6	48.2	37	24.2	8.3	0	2.2	18.2	30.2	113.5	130.2	143.6
136.2	117.6	100.4	81.7	65.1	50.1	38.2	56	97.8	89.1	76.3	66.3	53.3	39.9	28.7	15.9	0	8.3	10.5	26.5	38.5	105.3	121.9	135.3
120.3	101.7	84.5	65.8	49.2	34.2	22.3	40.1	81.9	73.2	60.4	50.4	37.4	24	12.8	0	15.9	24.2	26.4	42.4	54.4	89.4	106	119.4
107.5	88.9	71.7	53	36.4	21.4	9.5	27.3	69.1	60.4	47.6	37.6	24.6	11.2	0	12.8	28.7	37	39.2	55.2	67.2	76.6	93.2	106.6
99.8	81.2	64	45.3	28.7	13.7	1.8	16.1	57.9	49.2	36.4	26.4	13.4	0	11.2	24	39.9	48.2	50.4	66.4	78.4	68.9	85.5	98.9
113.2	94.6	77.4	58.7	42.1	27.1	15.2	19.3	44.5	35.8	23	13	0	13.4	24.6	37.4	53.3	61.6	63.8	79.8	91.8	82.3	98.9	112.3
126.2	107.6	90.4	71.7	55.1	40.1	28.2	32.3	31.5	22.8	10	0	13	26.4	37.6	50.4	66.3	74.6	76.8	92.8	104.8	95.3	111.9	125.3
136.2	117.6	100.4	81.7	65.1	50.1	38.2	42.3	21.5	12.8	0	10	23	36.4	47.6	60.4	76.3	84.6	86.8	102.8	114.8	105.3	121.9	135.3
149	130.4	113.2	94.5	77.9	62.9	51	55.1	8.7	0	12.8	22.8	35.8	49.2	60.4	73.2	89.1	97.4	99.6	115.6	127.6	118.1	134.7	148.1
157.7	139.1	121.9	103.2	86.6	71.6	59.7	63.8	0	8.7	21.5	31.5	44.5	57.9	69.1	81.9	97.8	106.1	108.3	124.3	136.3	126.8	143.4	156.8
116	97.4	80.2	61.4	44.8	29.8	17.9	0	63.8	55.1	42.3	32.3	19.3	16.1	27.3	40.1	56	64.3	66.5	82.5	94.5	85.1	101.7	115.1
98.1	79.5	62.3	43.5	26.9	11.9	0	17.9	59.7	51	38.2	28.2	15.2	1.8	9.5	22.3	38.2	46.5	48.7	64.7	76.7	67.2	83.8	97.2
86.2	67.6	50.4	31.6	15	0	11.9	29.8	71.6	62.9	50.1	40.1	27.1	13.7	21.4	34.2	50.1	58.4	60.6	76.6	88.6	55.3	71.9	85.3
71.2	52.6	35.4	16.6	0	15	26.9	44.8	86.6	77.9	65.1	55.1	42.1	28.7	36.4	49.2	65.1	73.4	75.6	91.6	103.6	40.3	56.9	70.3
54.6	36	18.8	0	16.6	31.6	43.5	61.4	103.2	94.5	81.7	71.7	58.7	45.3	53	65.8	81.7	90	92.2	108.2	120.2	23.7	40.3	53.7
35.8	17.2	0	18.8	35.4	50.4	62.3	80.2	121.9	113.2	100.4	90.4	77.4	64	71.7	84.5	100.4	108.7	110.9	126.9	138.9	4.9	21.5	34.9
18.6	0	17.2	36	52.6	67.6	79.5	97.4	139.1	130.4	117.6	107.6	94.6	81.2	88.9	101.7	117.6	125.9	128.1	144.1	156.1	12.3	28.9	42.3
0	18.6	35.8	54.6	71.2	86.2	98.1	116	157.7	149	136.2	126.2	113.2	99.8	107.5	120.3	136.2	144.5	146.7	162.7	174.7	30.9	47.5	60.9
13.9	32.5	49.7	68.5	85.1	100.1	112	129.9	171.6	162.9	150.1	140.1	127.1	113.7	121.4	134.2	150.1	158.4	160.6	176.6	188.6	44.8	61.4	74.8
25.5	44.1	61.3	80.1	96.7	111.7	123.6	141.5	183.2	174.5	161.7	151.7	138.7	125.3	133	145.8	161.7	170	172.2	188.2	200.2	56.4	73	86.4
30.7	49.3	66.5	85.3	101.9	116.9	128.8	146.7	188.4	179.7	166.9	156.9	143.9	130.5	138.2	151	166.9	175.2	177.4	193.4	205.4	61.6	78.2	91.6
108	126.6	143.8	162.6	179.2	194.2	206.1	224	265.7	257	244.2	234.2	221.2	207.8	215.5	228.3	244.2	252.5	254.7	270.7	282.7	138.9	155.5	168.9
99.9	118.5	135.7	154.5	171.1	186.1	198	215.9	257.6	248.9	236.1	226.1	213.1	199.7	207.4	220.2	236.1	244.4	246.6	262.6	274.6	130.8	147.4	160.8
87.8	106.4	123.6	142.4	159	174	185.9	203.8	245.5	236.8	224	214	201	187.6	195.3	208.1	224	232.3	234.5	250.5	262.5	118.7	135.3	148.7
76.2	94.8	112	130.8	147.4	162.4	174.3	192.2	236.9	225.2	212.4	202.4	189.4	176	183.7	196.5	212.4	220.7	222.9	238.9	250.9	107.1	123.7	137.1
63.2	81.8	99	117.8	134.4	149.4	161.3	179.2	220.9	212.2	199.4	189.4	176.4	163	170.7	183.5	199.4	207.7	209.9	225.9	237.9	94.1	110.7	124.1
49	67.6	84.8	103.6	120.2	135.2	147.1	165	206.7	198	185.2	175.2	162.2	148.8	156.5	169.3	185.2	193.5	195.7	211.7	223.7	79.9	96.5	109.9
51.7	70.3	87.5	106.3	122.9	137.9	149.8	167.7	209.4	200.7	187.9	177.9	164.9	151.5	159.2	172	187.9	196.2	198.4	214.4	226.4	82.6	99.2	112.6
52.3	80.9	98.1	116.7	135.5	152.1	160.4	178.3	220.1	211.4	198.6	188.6	175.6	162.2	169.9	182.7	198.6	206.9	209.1	225.1	237.1	93.2	109.8	123.2
30.9	99.5	116.7	135.5	152.1	167.1	179	196.9	238.6	229.9	217.1	207.1	194.1	180.7	188.4	201.2	217.1	225.4	227.6	243.6	254.6	111.8	128.4	141.8
44.6	163.2	180.4	199.2	215.8	230.8	242.7	260.6	302.3	293.6	280.8	270.8	257.8	244.4	252.1	264.9	280.8	289.1	291.3	307.3	319.3	175.5	192.1	205.5
135	153.6	170.8	189.6	206.2	221.2	233.1	251	292.7	284	271.2	261.2	248.2	234.8	242.5	255.3	271.2	279.5	281.7	297.7	309.7	165.9	182.5	195.9
20.2	138.8	156	174.8	191.4	206.4	218.3	236.2	277.9	269.2	256.4	246.4	233.4	220	227.7	240.5	256.4	264.7	266.9	282.9	294.9	151.1	167.7	181.1
37.9	116.5	133.7	152.5	169.1	184.1	196	213.9	255.6	246.9	234.1	224.1	211.1	197.7	205.4	218.2	234.1	242.4	244.6	260.6	272.6	128.8	145.4	158.8
76.8	95.4	112.6	131.4	148	163	174.9	192.8	234.5	225.8	213	203	190	176.6	184.3	197.1	213	221.3	223.5	239.5	251.5	107.7	124.3	137.7
30.9	99.5	116.7	135.5	152.1	167.1	179	196.9	238.6	229.9	217.1	207.1	194.1	180.7	188.4	201.2	217.1	225.4	227.6	243.6	255.6	111.8	128.4	141.8
96.1	114.7	131.9	150.7	167.3	182.3	194.2	212.1	253.8	245.1	232.3	222.3	209.3	195.9	203.6	216.4	232.3	240.6	242.8	258.8	270.8	127	143.6	157
106.1	124.7	141.9	160.7	177.3	192.3	204.2	222.1	263.8	255.1	242.3	232.3	219.3	205.9	213.6	226.4	242.3	250.6	252.8	268.8	280.8	137	153.6	167
110.1	128.7	145.9	164.7	181.3	196.3	208.2	226.1	267.8	259.1	246.3	236.3	223.3	209.9	217.6	230.4	246.3	254.6	256.8	272.8	284.8	141	157.6	171

Index of places

(A page number italicised refers to a map only)

Index of places

Index of places

USEFUL WEBSITES

www.cycle-west.com	Three new cycling routes - *basic information on the big routes - Velodyssey, Tour de Manche, etc*
www.af3v.org	Les véloroutes et voies vertes de France. *Useful for ideas but pay attention to the date of the information given*
www.base-plein-air-guerledan.com	Base Départementale de Plein Air de Guerlédan - *the website has a page for the Station VTT*
www.bretagne-rando.com	Walks and cycle circuits in Brittany - *interactive map to locate the walks*
www.brittanywalks.com	English language website on walking in Brittany - *includes an archive of articles, suggestions and information*
www.cfcb-asso.org	Association Chemins de Fer du Centre Bretagne - a railway preservation society - *excursions with preserved rolling stock and locomotives*
www.ter-sncf.com	TER (*trains express régionaux*) - *local trains that carry your bike free if there is room*
www.vtt-22.fr	Mountain biking in the department of Côtes d'Armor - *links to the Stations VTT*
www.rannerdale.co.uk	online cyclists' shop - books, maps, etc.
www.reddogbooks.com	Full details of all the Red Dog books - *with facility to buy online*

FURTHER READING

The Nantes-Brest Canal, a guide for walkers and cyclists - by Wendy Mewes. (Red Dog Books)

Réseau Breton, a Rail Network in Brittany - by Gordon Gravett. (The Oakwood Press)

Walks in Côtes d'Armor, Northern Brittany - by G.H.Randall (Red Dog Books)

Discovering the History of Brittany - by Wendy Mewes (Red Dog Books)

Cycling Northern France, cycle routes north of the Loire - by Richard Peace & Andrew Stevenson (Excellent Books)